Caregiver's Witness

—

A View of One Transplant

Marie Minarik

DEDICATION

For Jeff. We will see each other again.

CONTENTS

ACKNOWLEDGMENTS

My deepest appreciation goes to my dear friend-since-high-school, Victoria, for so painstakingly and lovingly editing this manuscript.

~~~

Having put a good bit of distance in terms of both time and miles between myself and the situation, the motivation to finally put my fingers to the keyboard came to me in the form of a gift from Jeff. You may believe whatever you choose, but there is zero question in my mind that he orchestrated this from his own private cloud, using his legendary iron will.

I'd been both consciously and unconsciously avoiding the effort of focusing on those days but was drawn to it by a series of events beyond myself. It began with my unexplained urgent craving for the fragrance of gardenias. Gardenia oil it had to be, but it's not easy to find. Thinking. They may have it at Pilgrim's Way, a metaphysical book store in Carmel-by-the-Sea. I called to check. We usually carry it, but haven't had any for a long time; it's very hard to get. Wait, a package from the manufacturer just arrived this morning. Let me take a look. And, yes, it's in there. I'll be over later today.

I arrived at Pilgrim's Way but gardenia oil wasn't on the shelf. I asked at the desk. Of course not, because it was still in the carton on the floor. And while the kind fellow was digging it out, a beautiful woman appeared at my side, holding a book about the language of flowers. She heard me ask for gardenia oil, and read to me about the meaning of gardenias. Peace, healing, relief from sorrow, etc. She asked if I had lost someone whose name begins with a G or a J. [What is happening to me?] Uh, yes, my husband, Jeff. With a J. She said he wants his story to be told.

As it turns out, at the same time that I was craving gardenia oil, the beautiful woman, Jann, and her husband, John, were relaxing in their Carmel-by-the-Sea hotel room during a journey from their home in Australia, en route to spending time with family in Texas. She said she felt a sudden strong urge to visit the very same book store and told John they had to go right away.

So the three of us talked for a few hours over two days. She knew so much about Jeff. It was a profound experience for me.

Gratefully accepting the gift of this strength, I give ultimate thanks both to Jeff and to Jann, my sister-in-spirit, who found me - not by chance - in "the place that begins with a C".

.

1 PROLOGUE

We hear or read it often, understanding the meaning but without noticing the words: "S/he died after a long battle with whatever-disease-or-condition". "Battle" is the operative word in that sentence, but maybe "war" would really be more apt.

"Battle" gives the impression of a one-time event, which is hardly accurate when describing dealing with a disease. Living with a disease is a whole string of battles - sometimes winning, sometimes losing - until the patient is either cured or not. The "war" continues every minute of every day and night. Sometimes there is a lot of action going on, sometimes there is a lull. The lulls can be more frightening than the action, because there is time to think about what is and worry about what is coming next, rather than simply reacting in the moment.

With disease, the war is usually a mystery to those not close to the patient. As the patient's wife and caregiver, I am telling this true story simply because it should be told. Whether you are a

1

transplant candidate, transplant recipient, caregiver, loved one, organ donor or family, or simply curious, it will give you an insight into the extremely atypical war that was one liver transplant.

2 MEET THE PATIENT

Let me introduce you to my husband, Thomas Jefferson "Jeff" Raney III, a prototype southern gentleman. He was human, of course, and he could be willful beyond comprehension, but he was at heart a truly good and extremely generous man.

More than one person described him as "larger than life". There was no missing him in a room. Physically, he was large: 6"4", 205 pounds. Very trim, not very muscular, but extremely strong. Well-schooled in "southern engineering", he was instinctively able to do things his size would not indicate. His booming voice was deep, with a distinctive Arkansas accent he never lost. His easy laugh was resounding. He was utterly unable to carry a tune; when I sang Happy Birthday, he would say that if he sang, too, the person would cry.

He was absolutely charming, kind and gracious to all, including those dreaded Customer Service Reps we all deal with via phone. He habitually addressed anyone with a name tag by their name; if they didn't have a tag, they were either Ma'am or Sir. He would converse with people on trains, in elevators, wherever. He wore his very soft heart on his sleeve.

At the same time, he was extremely tough emotionally. Having lost his father, mother and only brother in an automobile accident when he was in his late teens, he somehow found the inner strength to deal with it. The only times I ever witnessed him close to tears were each year on his brother's birthday. He was fond of saying that when something bad happens, you just have to put one foot in front of the other and keep walking.

On the topic of ethics and integrity, everything was black and white to Jeff. There was no compromise in this department.

Jeff was equally at home in his white dinner jacket or filthy work clothes. Perpetuating his military school discipline, he was meticulous in his dress. He lovingly polished his work shoes and briefcase to a mirror shine every Sunday evening. He ironed his jeans.

Things he particularly loved, besides life in general:

- Critters: horses (he grew up riding and showing), dogs, cats, birds, fish, cows, etc.
- Nature: trees and flowers (favorites were camellias and dogwoods), sunrises and sunsets, the seasons.
- Farms: his physician father also owned a cattle farm; Jeff did every type of physical farm labor himself.

- Music: particularly classical guitar and melodic jazz.

- Books: he was never without one, fiction or history mostly; "If it's not a hardback, it's not a book."

- Sailing: he loved being on the water, despite suffering from seasickness in very rough conditions; I once hoisted him 55' in the air to repair something on the top of a mast.

- Fountain pens: "A gentleman only writes with real ink from a bottle."

- Tools: "You can never have too many hammers."

- Hard work of any kind: absolutely nothing intimidated him (except electricity), and he threw himself into it, whether it was cleaning horse tack, digging holes for trees or bulbs, operating or repairing farm equipment, anything.

Jeff's love for his daughter, Christy, and son, TJ, who were grown and living in other states with their own families when I met him, was absolutely fierce, as was his love for me. There was no question in my mind that if anyone harmed any of us in any way, they would regret having done it.

No matter your perspective, he was quite a character, that guy. Born on April 1, 1945, he was 62 years old on the date of his transplant.

3 ESLD

ESLD. That would be End Stage Liver Disease. So what is that, exactly? Terminal, of course. Ominous, definitely. Scary, absolutely. It is all that. But just what happens to the one who is stricken?

Since I am a lay person, this explanation is from my simplistic level of understanding. The liver is the main part of the body's waste management system. Basically, it purifies the blood. When the liver doesn't work, the body poisons itself. The ultimate result is death, but death is nothing compared to what comes before. I'm going to tell you about what Jeff experienced, only omitting the gorier details. It turned out to be a very long road. *Jeff's case was absolutely __not__ typical;* it's just one scenario.

For over 15 years before I met Jeff, he had known his liver was not quite OK. They picked up on it during a routine blood test. One of his liver enzyme levels (alkaline phosphatase or "alk phos") was elevated. That was the first indicator.

Not a huge deal at this point, the Gastroenterologist said. Your liver function is not quite normal. It could stay just like this and you could live a fine, long life for years and years. Or not. We have no idea why this is happening to you, so we call it "idiopathic". Your case is extremely unusual. You don't abuse alcohol. You've never used IV drugs. You have never had hepatitis. For the record, we'll identify it as "autoimmune cholangiopathy with overlap". In lay language this means that your immune system is attacking both your liver and gall bladder. There are very few, maybe a handful, of people like you out there. We will just watch it closely and treat it if and when the disease progresses. So Jeff took a drug every day for years and went on with his life.

Things did stay the same for years and he felt just fine, but then changes started to happen and the rate of deterioration accelerated as time passed. By the fall of 2006, Jeff started to both look and act differently.

From the looks perspective, his color gradually changed. First his complexion started to pale, then it became extremely pale. Jaundice, (yellow skin and the whites of the eyes), is a prime symptom of liver failure. In Jeff's case, even by the time he was close to death, jaundice was never very dramatic as it is in some people, but he did develop a definite yellowish tone.

Another physical symptom was edema, which is when the cells retain fluid and swell. What do you do about edema? The first action is limiting sodium intake. Sodium is in almost everything, so it

7

isn't easy to do. The next tactic is taking diuretics. First, Jeff's feet got puffy. Then his ankles. Then his lower legs, and it progressed upwards from there. It started out to be only in the morning, but then it became constant. Early on, it was just inconvenient, but later it became one of the more intractable and extremely uncomfortable manifestations.

The edema was definitely affected by his sodium intake. For a guy who always loved and craved salty foods, to the extent of salting ham sandwiches, this was a daily trial. Un-salty foods just didn't taste good to him. He tried and grudgingly adopted the use of salt substitute. Did this work? At the onset, it did help a little, but as time passed it was not nearly sufficient. Eventually, his shoes didn't come close to fitting. There was no way he could even get his socks on. We tried sox for "big" men, but not even those would fit. He started wearing either slippers or his favorite Birkenstock sandals with the straps let all the way out. His feet and ankles looked like rubber gloves blown up beyond capacity. And not only did they look uncomfortable, they were actually painful, and affected his ability to walk. When you think about edema, it doesn't seem as though it would be a big deal, but let me tell you, in terms of quality of life, it is.

As bad as Jeff's edema was, it paled when compared to ascites (pronounced "a-SITE-ease"). Unless you have either had, or known someone who has had, liver disease, you may not know that ascites is fluid accumulation in the abdominal cavity. He looked as if he were very, very pregnant and about to burst open. And that included his genitals, if you can possibly imagine such a sight. We bought very large athletic supporters to help make him a little more comfortable. And he used a lot of baby powder. Nothing helped to any degree. Needless to say, his underwear and slacks didn't fit. And when we bought some that would close around his waist, he looked like Tweedle Dee. This was an ongoing nightmare in every respect, particularly because since he was very fastidious about his grooming, it upset him to see how his appearance had become affected.

He was extremely uncomfortable in every position, 24 hours of every single day.

So what do they do about ascites? That's not simple, either. First, since fluid is just floating freely around inside the abdominal cavity, diuretics don't help. The only way to remove it is in a hospital, by sticking a fat needle into one of the fluid-filled spaces and draining it out. They call this "tapping". Actually, they don't so much draw it out as just let it flow or squirt out, as it would if you stuck a hole into a water-filled balloon. Besides being uncomfortable, the fluid is a prime infection source, but the more they intervene to remove it, the less the body will do to prevent it from re-accumulating. In other words, the more fluid they take, the more the body will produce. Plus, the very act of removing it can cause even more serious problems, including puncturing something or causing infection. So they make each decision to tap based on the overall picture at the moment. In Jeff's case, he was tapped at least three times. Usually this is done as an outpatient. Once while I sat there and watched, over the course of an hour Jeff gave up 10 liters (i.e., more than 2 ½ gallons) of fluid that looked like weak tea. They could have taken even more, but they stopped because, well, what's the use?

The last major aspect, which was not obvious to someone who saw him, was hepatic encephalopathy. This means that because the brain is receiving dirty blood from the sick liver, it stops working normally. So what? Motor skills are affected, for one thing. He walked strangely and fell a number of times. His handwriting became illegible. General brain function deteriorated, including memory, personality, etc. Jeff became a different person: one with a pretty healthy degree of dementia. For me, this was completely unsettling, even frightening sometimes. I can't even begin to know what it was like for him; he never talked about it. I can only hope he wasn't aware then and didn't remember later.

So now you have a teeny window into what ELSD really means and what life is like for those who suffer, whether it's their own fault because of their behaviors, or not. It's ugly, slow torture, and the most daunting aspect of all is that every minute you wonder how much worse it will get before it's finally over.

4 THE LIVER TRANSPLANT PROCESS

For a lucky few there is the miracle of transplant. There are never enough organs for everyone whose livers are failing, so a decision has to be made as to who is most likely to benefit long term. That assessment includes not only the liver itself, but the overall health of the patient as well as their behaviors and habits, because after a transplant the recipient must comply with ongoing drug therapy, including follow-up visits and periodic blood tests for the rest of their lives.

Another aspect is the caregiver. The patient can't do it alone. Someone has to be available to support the patient after surgery, throughout recovery, and going forward. It's a huge commitment given the best of circumstances.

I'm not going to address financial considerations, but suffice it to say that without insurance, it would not be an option for any but the wealthiest among us.

When a doctor determines that a patient may potentially need a transplant, the first step is to be evaluated by the Transplant Team at the chosen hospital. In our case, this was The Hospital of the University of Pennsylvania ("HUP"), one of the premier transplant hospitals. The Team includes a number of different specialist physicians and surgeons, a Transplant Coordinator (a specially-trained nurse who will work with the patient throughout the process), and someone from finance. Jeff and I spent a whole day with members of the Team, being thoroughly interviewed to assess whether, in fact, he would be an acceptable candidate.

Once the patient is approved, the patient then goes onto the nationwide Transplant List for that organ (or organs, in some cases). The List, which changes moment by moment, includes those from the very sickest at the top, to the least sick at the bottom.

The United Network for Organ Sharing (UNOS), is the entity that sets the policies for liver transplants. The process works differently depending on the organ. For livers, the critical measurement is called the Model End-stage Liver Disease ("MELD") Score, which supposedly reflects how sick the patient is. Everyone admits it's not perfect, but it's the fairest measurement that exists. A patient's MELD Score is calculated arithmetically using results of blood tests. The patient's initial MELD Score determines the patient's starting position on the Transplant List.

Then periodic blood tests begin. Over time, as the patient's disease worsens and their MELD Score gets higher, blood tests are required more frequently. When the MELD Score reaches a certain level, UNOS notifies the Gift of Life Foundation to begin the process of trying to find an organ for transplant. It's worth mentioning that if a patient stops showing up for required blood tests, they are dropped from the List.

In the case of liver transplants, the criteria for matching an organ are simple: blood type and organ size. The ideal organ would be whole, which means that it would come from a deceased person. Having said that, the liver is the only organ that regenerates, meaning that if part is removed from a living person, what's left will re-grow the missing part. So, it's possible that someone could donate part of their liver to someone else. For a patient sick enough to need a transplant, the strain of receiving a partial liver and having to grow the rest is not the best situation, but if there is no whole organ available it can mean the difference between life and death. I was dumbfounded to learn that when someone donates part of their liver, the removed part grows back in six weeks. That's right. Just six weeks.

Needless to say, many people die while awaiting transplants because an organ isn't available when it's needed. The other aspect is the physical location of the patient and the organ. A harvested organ can only last for a few hours before being transplanted.

The Gift of Life Foundation is the 24x7x365 organization that matches organs with patients and coordinates the logistics. I had the privilege of visiting their local site years later. My jaw literally dropped when I saw the room full of people in cubicles, on phones, watching a very large real-time electronic board listing the vitals. The closest thing I could compare it to would be an airport control tower. The emotional enormity reduced me to tears.

The most common situation is that the patient would be close to home, with a beeper, awaiting word that an organ has been found. The patient must be ready to get to the hospital immediately or forfeit the organ.

When a potential match is made, the organ is assessed to confirm suitability for the patient. If, for whatever reason, it isn't acceptable, the search begins again. There could potentially be many false alarms before a transplant takes place. It's a huge emotional roller-coaster ride.

After liver transplant surgery, the average hospital stay is nine to fourteen days. As you will see, this was not Jeff's experience.

It's important to note that the vast majority of transplants are anonymous, meaning that neither the donor nor the recipient are told the identity of the other. If, after a transplant, the recipient is open to learning the identity of the donor, the recipient can contact the Gift of Life Foundation, which will, in turn, contact the donor. If the donor is open to it, the Gift of Life Foundation will pass on the information. What happens then is up to the two parties. Another post-transplant service the Gift of Life Foundation provides is forwarding an anonymous letter from the recipient to the donor, giving the recipient the opportunity to express their gratitude. Try taking a deep breath to imagine what you might actually write if you were in this position.

What does the whole process feel like emotionally? What Jeff and I experienced was the extreme of the extreme, and it was completely different for each of us. I, unfortunately for me sometimes, remained awake and alert throughout, while Jeff was totally mentally unaware for a great deal of the time. He had the blessing of never recalling much of his ordeal. Later, he did not wish to know, because it would have been too difficult to endure.

Having said that, being a patient awaiting a transplant or being their caregiver is stressful in so many ways. There is worry, frustration, and uncertainty. Hopes are raised, then dashed. The norm is wait, then hurry up. There is a total lack of control. There are ups and downs, even in the smoothest of cases. The best news is that there are plenty of people ready and willing to provide support, whether or not it is requested.

Lastly, even if things go without a hitch, no transplant is without an ultimate price. Extended drug therapies come with side-effects, some of which are awful. The combination of the ordeal and the meds can result in personality changes, not to mention physical challenges. Once there is an ESLD diagnosis, life will never be the same.

5 JEFF'S SITUATION

Jeff's overall physical constitution was extremely complex and unique. It was clear to everyone involved that his personal MELD Score was not an accurate representation of just how sick he was. Regardless, the MELD Score was the controlling factor so we had no choice but to watch and wait.

We did, in fact, have one option. When a patient is on the Transplant List, it's permissible to be a candidate at more than one hospital, assuming the patient can get there quickly enough if an organ is found. Jeff's Transplant Team suggested we also consider the Mayo Clinic in Jacksonville, Florida, which for some reason was able to transplant at a lower MELD Score. We investigated and did start making plans to go to Florida and to stay there if possibilities seemed better than at HUP. We expected it wouldn't be long before he got a transplant, then roughly two weeks' recovery, then we could come home and use HUP going forward. As it happened, because of Jeff's overall health, we never had to act on that plan. This turned out to be a blessing.

As time passed and Jeff was worsening, his Primary Care Physician ("PCP") told us that there were more than sufficient diagnoses to admit Jeff to HUP, so it would be up to Jeff to speak up when he felt he would rather be in the hospital than at home. On February 16, 2007, Jeff was feeling particularly sick and downhearted. He sat on the sofa with his head in his hands, and did something 100% contrary to his nature: he gave up. He said it was time to go. I stopped crying long enough to alert the PCP, and call both his daughter, Christy, and son, TJ. We rushed to the ER for admission. He would now wait there for whatever happened first: either his MELD Score would elevate enough for a transplant, or he would die.

Instinctively I realized that the only reasonable, effective, and selfish way for me to keep relatives and friends current would be to send a regular mass eMail. That way everyone would get the same information and I would be spared endless repetitions on the phone. My daily routine was to feed the cats and the fish in our pond, work from home for eight hours, drive to HUP, spend time with Jeff and talk with the Transplant Team, drive home, then write the eMail, either before or after getting whatever sleep I could.

During Jeff's hospital stay, I learned three cardinal facts:

1)   A jillion things beep, incessantly and relentlessly, in hospital rooms. Get used to it.

2) Everything depends on something else. The D-word ("depends") always rules.

3) Absolutely everything is subject to change at any moment.

The eMails follow...

6 THE EMAIL JOURNAL

2/20/2007 Update for All

The doctor said late yesterday afternoon that Jeff is "responding to treatment" for peritonitis but won't say when or whether he can go home. I asked if it might be today and he was non-committal. I also broached the subject about the possibility of a transplant at HUP. The doctor said that the UNOS regulations strictly govern their transplants, and that at 11, Jeff's MELD Score isn't high enough for HUP. He said that we should proceed with the Mayo process as an alternative. Amen.

Jeff is extremely whooped, but he doesn't look as sick as he did before admission. He's happy to be in HUP, so that tells me he needs to be there.

xxoo M'ree

∞

2/21/2007   Improvement

Jeff is responding to antibiotics. He's very weak and they are working on having him eat at least some food and also drink a liquid high-nutritional diet supplement. They're changing his meds and will do more tests and probably another tap today. He may come home in the next couple of days.

I'm on auto pilot, but am sleeping thanks to a homeopathic sleep aid. Good stuff!

xxoo M'ree

∞

2/22/2007   Wednesday Update

Jeff's peritonitis is under control now and if he were stronger he could come home. He's so thin and weak that he can barely sit up. We have to force him to eat. He won't answer the phone, which is completely unlike him. You get the picture. There is no way I could manage to care for him at home in this state, even if I didn't have to work. So they are looking for a rehab facility for him, and when they find one, they will move him. Then as soon as he is stronger, he can actually come home. That will be a good day.

xxoo M'ree

∞

2/23/2007 Jeff Update

Jeff is still at HUP. He is still extremely weak. Actually, the medical evaluations say he is even weaker than he appears. They decided not to send him to a rehab facility, because in those places you must have at least three hours of PT every day, and Jeff can't do nearly that much. They are looking for a "skilled nursing facility", where he will get PT, but less than three hours a day. When they find one, they will move him. Meanwhile, the nurses had him sitting up having lunch yesterday when I arrived at 2pm. That's a good step.

Both Christy and TJ will be coming up to spend a few days in March. Maybe together; maybe separately. A visit will be good for Jeff and his kids. I'll enjoy their company, too.

And for something to look forward to, Christy said that after Jeff has his new liver, she and her husband are going to give us their Key West timeshare for a week. Wooohoooo! I'm already there in my mind.

xxoo M'ree

∞

2/26/2007 Moving Day is Tuesday

The plan is that Jeff may be moved to a nearby skilled nursing facility tomorrow. Looks like a very nice place, as these places go. It's 4.5 miles / 12 minutes away from our house, so that's super. If and when he gets stronger, he can come home.

Also, since his MELD score has suddenly rocketed up to 25, the next thing is that HUP doctors are supposed to call the Mayo doctors. We may be going to Florida soon. Stay tuned.

xxoo M'ree

∞

2/27/2007   Jeff Update: No Move

Plans to move Jeff have been put on hold because his kidneys are now acting up. They are doing tests and I should know more tomorrow.

Christy and TJ are both coming up from March 15th to the 19th, assuming we are not in Florida.

xxoo M'ree

∞

2/28/2007   Would You Believe No News Today?

Only the doctor from the general medicine team visited while I was there, so I only know they are continuing to do tests for Jeff's kidney function. Actually, he seemed much more relaxed today. One of the tests involved giving him IV fluids, which seems to have made him more comfortable. He ate (actually, I fed him) some chicken and rice soup, and he drank a whole bottle of a high-protein nutritional supplement. That's real progress. He did not get out of bed; they have a catheter installed now. They cancelled the GI Doctor's appointment that had been scheduled for today.

I'm going to sleep tonight for a change.

xxoo M'ree

∞

3/2/2007   No Liver This Time

Jeff's MELD Score is now high enough to do a transplant at HUP. Yesterday afternoon they told us that they may have located a donor liver, and that they would be preparing him for surgery, assuming things would be a go. My heart started racing with anticipation and I called the kids.

At 1:30am, they told me that this liver was too small for Jeff. Oh, no! It's back to the List for Jeff. I'm home to sleep. Maybe next time...

Thanks, everyone, for your care and concern and support. Special thanks to those of you who have been feeding the cats and fish while I've been at HUP. They are just fine.

xxoo M'ree

∞

3/3/2007   Update From Friday

Things are about the same. We're waiting for the next liver. While we are so disappointed that the first one was too small, I'm so encouraged that the time is finally here.

The GI Doctors said it's most likely he will not go to Florida since he's now so high on the list here. The Kidney Doctors are watching carefully and strongly believe that the kidney issues are caused by the liver issues, and that as soon as he has a transplant, everything will clear up. The GI Doctors agree with that. It is possible that if it takes long to find a liver, he may need dialysis, but this is premature speculation. The nurses are taking excellent care of him and do a great job keeping him comfortable.

He's very sick, extremely weak and pretty out of it, but he's eating what I feed him and drinking a lot. They are giving him IV fluids to keep him hydrated, which also goes a long way to keeping him comfortable. Whenever he needs it, they will tap his belly again.

Barring other developments, I'm set to take vacation days while Christy and TJ are here so we can all be together.

The liver call could come at any minute. It's completely surreal to think about the donors and their families while we sit and wait. We will never know who to thank.

xxoo M'ree

∞

3/4/2007 – 3/5/2007 (*not an eMail*) - **My Own Experience**

It is important for you to know what I experienced during the day prior to Jeff's transplant as well as on the day of surgery.

I waited as Jeff's condition deteriorated literally by the minute. He was in and out of lucidity and/or sleep, but he was always conscious. I was teetering on the edge of composure.

In the late afternoon, someone told me they believed they found a second potential liver, but that, even if it worked out, it would probably be at least a full day before surgery.

By about 10pm there was still no update. My mind was racing. I knew if tomorrow was to be transplant day, some things needed doing in advance, including feeding the cats and fish, a shower for me, a change of clothes, notifying my office, etc. I asked Jeff's Nurse if it would be safe for me to go home for about two hours. She assured me there was plenty of time for that, and to maybe get a couple hours of sleep before coming back. I gathered my things, gave Jeff a kiss, and made my way from the hospital to the parking garage. Since the pedestrian bridge between the buildings was already closed and locked up for the night, I had to get Security to let me out.

At the very instant I was unlocking my car, my cell phone rang. It was Jeff's Nurse. She said they were taking him to surgery NOW, and I should get back immediately to see him off. It was like a movie, with the world going in slow motion while my heart pounded. I literally dropped my stuff and ran back across the bridge. I had to call Security to let me back into the hospital and up to his floor. When I got off the elevator, they were already wheeling his gurney down the hall. I ran to catch up with them, gave Jeff a quick kiss goodbye, and collapsed onto the closest chair. Jeff's Nurse apologized, explaining that this liver was, in fact, a match and that the timeframe had sped up. She told me he would be in surgery for at least 10 hours, and that now it was really safe to go home. I should go directly to the Family Waiting Room outside of the surgical suites when I returned.

It was impossible to avoid thinking about the drama taking place. The donor's family grieving. The surgeons removing the donor's liver. Jeff being prepared to receive it. It was completely surreal. Tears flowed down my face with so many emotions: relief, sadness, hopefulness, emotional exhaustion.

I got back to HUP by about 5am and Security had to let me back inside. When I arrived in the Family Waiting Room, I was immediately reassured and was able to calm down. It was a very large, mostly open-floor-plan suite of areas, including very comfortable seating areas (some with TV, some quiet), areas with computers and phones, refreshment areas, and private discussion rooms. The reception desk was staffed with nurses. They took my cell number so they could contact me if I went anywhere else, say, to the cafeteria. There were large hanging monitors for patient status. Each patient had a line, with the first two letters of their first name, then first two letters of their last name (for confidentiality), as well as columns for times: operating room in, surgery start, recovery room in, and out. The lines scrolled like an airport flight status board. The best thing was that there were nurses assigned to make periodic rounds of the operating rooms, gather data about each patient, and come back to give personal updates to waiting families. I knew it would be a long day, so I had my knitting rather than a book. Who could concentrate to read anything?

During the day, the drama continued non-stop. Some families were in and out quickly. Some were there for very long periods. It was obvious who was there for serious situations. Doctors would come in and take families into private rooms. There were tears and there were celebrations. I just waited, sometimes knitting, sometimes not. Updates for me were very encouraging. Things were going smoothly, but slowly. I took notes because there was no way I would remember anything. I was brain dead.

And all of the staff do this every day. It's normal to them.

∞

3/6/2007   No Jaundice- No Belly

Maybe I was just overly tired by 6:30 last night, but I could swear I had a husband transplant yesterday. The way gorked-out guy in the Surgical Intensive Care Unit ("SICU") sort of looks like Jeff, but he's not yellow and his belly is flat. Maybe my eyes were just worn out from no sleep and too many crying spells. Anyway, now I've had a few hours of deep sleep, so I'll check carefully today and report back.

Here's what happened, according to my notes:

3:30am Jeff was taken from his room to the operating room for prep.

9:00   Anesthesia was started.

9:47   They removed 15 liters of fluid from his belly and started the surgery.

1:40pm The old liver was out; it took longer than they expected because his veins were stiff from many years of disease.

3:00   The new liver was in and they were doing all the other things they had to do.

4:30   The Transplant Surgeon came in person to tell me that the surgery was over and give me more information. The new liver is a good one and is doing its job beautifully. There was a clot in his portal vein, which they removed, but it's not as perfect as they would like. They will do an ultrasound later and may have to do a small surgery to work on it tomorrow. They didn't try to repair the hernia left over from his prior abdominal surgery because it was just too much to do; we can do that any time. They were taking him to the SICU and I could see him as soon as he was properly situated.

6:30   They let me visit Jeff and a bunch of the Transplant Team members introduced themselves to me. They seemed like normal people but that just couldn't be. I looked closely, but didn't see evidence of wings. Jeff was totally zonked out and on a ventilator. They had done an ultrasound and the portal vein was now fine. I held his hand and wished him pleasant dreams.

The doctors told me that Jeff had been "hours from death" at the time of the transplant. The heck with Disney Land. I am going to a hot bubble bath followed by dreamland.

xxoo M'ree
Organ Donors Save Lives

∞

3/7/2007   No Jaundice - No Belly - and I Wasn't Dreaming

All that stuff yesterday was really real.

Jeff is doing very, very well. The portal vein clot has disappeared. At 3:30 yesterday afternoon they removed the ventilator and he let the nurses know very clearly that it wasn't a pleasant experience. They laughed out loud. They understand it's not his usual demeanor. They said they are concerned when a patient doesn't react much.

When Jeff was admitted on February 16th, he weighed 225 lbs. He is now 190.3 lbs. If you asked my opinion, I would say that he looks like much less than that.

If he keeps improving, later today they will move him from the SICU to a room on the Transplant Floor. Then he can have adult visitors, providing they are 100% healthy. The next thing to go will be the nasal-gastric ("NG") tube [for feeding - it goes through the nose into the stomach], maybe in another day.

I slept like a baby for 11 hours last night and feel almost normal today; it's been so long I'm not exactly sure what "normal" feels like. I'm thrilled that my friend from Seattle, Pammie, is arriving this afternoon to stay until Monday. Christy and TJ will arrive next Thursday to stay until the following Monday. It will be great for them to see him and vice versa.

xxoo M'ree
Organ Donors Save Lives

∞

3/8/2007   Recovering

When I got to the SICU yesterday, Jeff's NG tube was gone and he was more awake. It's often hard to understand what he says, but somehow he gets his messages across. He was allowed to have some water. He says he does not have pain.

His heart is sometimes irregular, but that is not so unusual. The doctors expect that the irregularity will disappear as he recovers, as he has never before had any heart issues. They are monitoring him carefully and are medicating him for it. Also, his right lung is partially collapsed and he has a lot of secretions in both his lungs.

This is also not so unusual and is not concerning them overly. They have a Respiratory Therapist working on him regularly with percussions (pounding on the back of his chest to loosen secretions) and coughing (to remove what is loosened). Because of these things, Jeff will be in the SICU for at least another day.

There is a constant parade of doctors and nurses, each doing their own thing and talking to all the others. It strikes me like an ant colony.

I left at 3:30 to pick Pammie up at the airport. It's great to have her here and we did a lot of talking before we crashed for the night.

At 3am I was jolted awake by the phone ringing. The doctor told me that Jeff had some bleeding from his nose and that his platelets were low. They put him back on the ventilator to prevent pneumonia. He said that Jeff was more comfortable with it than without it. They didn't want me to be alarmed when I arrived in the morning. They are SO good at what they do.

xxoo M'ree
Organ Donors Save Lives

∞

3/9/2007   "Minor Setbacks"

The end first. Jeff is still in the SICU. The Transplant Team assured me that Jeff is only experiencing "minor setbacks", that his issues are relatively easily managed, and that "we aren't even close to

31

thinking" that his kids should come earlier than their scheduled arrival next Thursday. The Team understands that I can't always interpret what is going on and would need notice if the situation becomes critical enough to summon the kids.

He's still on the ventilator, but he is doing most of the work and they are periodically lowering the oxygen level. They may be able to remove it today. His right lung is still partially collapsed and full of secretions and they will suction it again. The whole objective is to prevent pneumonia. His nostrils are packed with gauze because he had a bleed which they couldn't stop because his platelets are low. His heart rhythm is starting to stabilize, but they are still medicating him for that. His kidney function is not good, but they are giving him more diuretics to help. They were going to give him a couple of units of blood, which should also help his kidneys. Only one of the three surgical drains is still remaining, which is a good thing. As of this morning, he will be started on custom-blended IV nutrition. The nutritionist told me that given that he weighed 190.3 out of surgery, considering the fluids on board, he probably actually weighs more like 150-160 now. They want to start fattening him up, but they don't want any food in his stomach yet. And, oh, the new liver is still functioning perfectly.

He is responsive, as much as someone can be while on a ventilator. He says he is not in pain. Jeff's Nurse said it was ok for Pammie to come in for a minute, and Jeff nodded that he wanted to see her. He squeezed her hand.

I slept like a baby last night.

xxoo M'ree
Organ Donors Save Lives

∞

3/10/2007   Improvement

Yesterday brought much improvement, although he's still in the SICU on the ventilator with his arms restrained so he doesn't try to pull it out consciously or unconsciously. He is alert and responsive when he is not sleeping. The liver is perfect. He's still getting pain meds, but they must be sufficient because he says he has no pain. The packings are still in his nose, including the long strings hanging out. It looks very weird.

Lungs: They had suctioned him again before I arrived and the subsequent x-ray showed that the offending right lung was almost totally clear. His breathing is now much less labored. They are continuing to reduce the oxygen level in the ventilator, but he still needs the support it provides. No trace of pneumonia.

Heart: They switched his meds and his heart rate is now stable.

Kidneys: They had given him two units of blood and increased his diuretics. He's now "peeing like a racehorse", as Jeff would say if he could talk. Excellent progress, and quickly, too.

Nutrition: They are giving him IV nutrition that looks like a vanilla milkshake. It's full of the important stuff, including amino acids, trace minerals, protein, etc. They said that they may soon start giving him something via the tube in his mouth.

The Wound Care Nurse was in there for a long time fussing about and making sure that everything about his exterior was absolutely perfect, all the time explaining everything she was doing. She changed all the bandages on his arms and tended to each of his many skin tears. She removed the blood pressure cuff so it wouldn't irritate his skin unnecessarily and said that the other nurses would just have to put it on and then take it off every hour. She adjusted the ventilator taping so it wouldn't irritate his mouth or pull on his beard. She used special tools to clean his mouth, brush his teeth, suction his throat and moisturize the whole area. She rolled towels and propped his head and arms and legs so he would both stay comfortable and not end up sliding down in the bed. She said she likes a clean bed so she changed the linens again and wiped down the whole apparatus. Go, go, go!

The Transplant Team came in, all smiles. They ordered that someone put in a few stitches around the lone remaining drain so it wouldn't seep fluids. They said they are very encouraged and looking for "one more day of stability". Until what, I didn't even think to ask; probably transferring him out of the SICU. At this point they have demonstrated that they are on top of every detail. I trust that they will do whatever is needed at the right moment and that they will tell me everything.

The awful worry and pressure is melting away. Jeff still looks pretty sorry being so skinny and blotched everywhere with vivid purple bruises, but I know he will be ok.

xxoo M'ree
Organ Donors Save Lives

∞

3/11/2007   Improvement?

Since yesterday was Saturday, the normal active SICU routine with tons of doctors around was different. All the nurses and respiratory people were there, but relatively few doctors. Jeff's situation is the same. Still on the ventilator, still no pain, still pretty generally gorked. Actually, if you asked me, I would say he was somewhat more gorked than the day before. He slept a lot of the time and was not quite as quick to respond either. All the vital systems are doing fine.

One notable and very disconcerting event. When I arrived, Jeff's nose packings had disappeared. This was fine until about an hour later, when a pretty healthy amount of blood started seeping out of his mouth and soaking the pillow. Jeff's Nurse immediately turned off the heparin drip and called the Resident, who came running. The Resident called the Transplant Team, who very quickly sent one of their Doctors. It seems they are working to find the fine heparin balance that will satisfy the liver transplant need while not causing other bleeding. The blood from his mouth was actually coming from

35

the back of his nose. The packings went right back in, where they are likely to remain for maybe even a week.

Also, in addition to the IV nutrition, they are now giving him "feeding trials". This means that once in a while they put extra nutrition (different from the other; this one looks like a butterscotch milkshake) into his stomach via a throat tube. Then they check somehow to see if the stomach processes it. This will tell them when he will be ready to eat normally. Of course, as long as he's on the ventilator, there will be no eating as we know it.

I'm expecting that today, Sunday, will be similarly quiet. Last night I noticed feeling as if I may be coming down with a cold/throat thing. At this moment I don't think so but will wait to see how the morning goes. If I am even remotely concerned that I might even possibly be even starting to get even a teeny bit sick, I can't go into his room. This would upset me.

Lastly, to give all the hospital staff an idea of how Jeff looked before he became a patient, I've hung a photo in his room. It shows us before some formal event, with him in his white dinner jacket. The transformation is jarring.

xxoo M'ree
Organ Donors Save Lives

∞

3/12/2007   Thank Goodness for No Brain Bleed

False alarm: I'm not sick. But Jeff is. Yesterday when I arrived, Jeff was looking, well, very sick. That's because on Saturday evening he developed a fever and by the time I arrived it was 101.7. His eyes looked glassy, like a person's do when they have a fever. He was virtually unresponsive, which was very disconcerting, to say the least. I say virtually because he did move around when his Nurse washed his eyes and mouth with saline. Otherwise, he didn't respond to anything else the entire time I was there. I have no idea if he even knew that I was in the room. They had him on extra antibiotics and were also culturing both his blood and urine to see if they could figure out exactly what it was and then target the drugs.

Because he was unresponsive and also because he had the nose bleeding episode the day before, they wanted to be positive that nothing had happened in his brain, so after I left for the day they did a head CAT scan, which showed no brain bleed. At least he's only sick.

All his other systems are doing great, including his stomach and digestive tract. When they feel it's safe to try again, which may be today, they will remove the nose packings. Then if there is no bleeding for a day after that, they plan to remove the ventilator. I'm hoping that he's at least off the ventilator when his kids arrive so he can talk to them.

Pammie is leaving early this evening, so I will take her to the airport on the way home from HUP. She did get to poke her head in on both Thursday and Friday, but not since then. Who knows what today will bring?

xxoo M'ree
Organ Donors Save Lives

∞

3/13/2007   Up and Down

Jeff's fever was almost gone when I arrived yesterday, but he was only a little responsive throughout the day. He opened and closed his eyes once in a while, but that was about it. I don't think he realized that I was there. The Neurologists were all over him like a cheap suit, as he would say. They did more than an hour of physical tests and an EEG. He didn't do too well with the physical tests, but the EEG was negative. Net is that they believe his mental status is due to an electrolyte imbalance. They are working hard to balance them by changing meds and increasing fluids. They are pretty confident that this will bring him back fairly quickly.

Nose packing is still in, but they may take it out today. After that, they hope to get him off the ventilator.

The Cardio Team came in to reassure me that despite another small rhythm issue the night before, everything is ok. The Kidney Team came in to check him out and let me know that his kidney issues are up and down but generally resolving. The Transplant Team visited and they remain very positive. They stressed that he was very sick going into surgery and that his surgery was very difficult. They hadn't told me until now that they needed three surgeons for most of it because of his vein condition.

Jeff's situation is already way far from typical and is a medical mystery to the staff; they have said that explicitly. Now a lightbulb moment. I've finally internalized a complicated concept that should be obvious but wasn't to me. The staff takes one step at a time and deals with what is as it happens. I don't know what I don't know. The staff doesn't know what I don't know, either, but their focus is on the patient, not on me. They don't always remember to make sure I understand the implications of each thing that is going on. I need to ask whatever questions I have when I have them. If I don't ask, shame on me.

I'm also learning that each team has their own subtle ways of saying "Don't worry. We're on it. He'll be fine." I need to be alert for those messages for my own reassurance.

Pammie left without seeing Jeff again. I have been blessed to have her as my temporary guardian angel and general distraction wizard. His kids will arrive later this week. At their request I'm making a To-Do-Around-The-House list for them.

xxoo M'ree
Organ Donors Save Lives

∞

3/13/2007   Waking Up Somewhat

Today there's been a big improvement. Jeff was sometimes awake and he knew I was there. They now attribute the mental status issue to kidney failure (which caused the electrolyte imbalance), which is resolving nicely with their attention.

He is totally off the pain meds and heparin. They were taking the nose packings out when I arrived at 11am and he didn't bleed. His heart has been fine. His lungs are good and when he is more awake, which may even be later tonight, they will extubate him. He must be fully conscious so his body remembers to breathe. In addition to the IV nutrition, his wonderful Nurse was pushing extra liquid nutrition through his oral tube so that if they extubate him, he will at least have something in his stomach until they actually expect him to eat food. If I'm not present when they extubate him, the nurses promised to tell me everything he says. They said the last episode was the most entertaining they ever heard. I can just imagine.

The orthotics person brought special boots for his feet and ankles. They look like Halloween costume space boots made of plastic, foam and Velcro. They are intended to keep his heels from rubbing on the bed and also to keep his hips from splaying out. They went right on top of the periodically-automatic-inflating lower leg wraps that keep him from getting leg clots. I didn't mention the wraps before, but he's had those since the transplant.

I also got to see his incision. It's gorgeous, if something like that can be gorgeous. It's like a big inverted, spread out Y, starting right under his sternum down for about four inches, with the legs extending almost eight inches or so to the sides. It's all smooth and stapled, with no swelling at all. The last drain is still in, but not much is draining.

He's progressing in the right direction. I'm progressing in the direction of a bubble bath followed by deep sleep.

xxoo M'ree
Organ Donors Save Lives

∞

3/15/2007   Just In Case I Was Relaxing Too Much

Oh, yesterday was so scary.

When I arrived at the hospital, Jeff was still intubated, not very aware, and looking very whooped. His Nurse rushed in to tell me that he'd had a bad night. At about 1am, his blood oxygen level had dropped, despite the respirator. He'd had a large amount of "stuff" in his lungs again, which had probably accumulated over time. They'd had to remove the ventilator, anesthetize him and "bronch" him, which means they stuck a big tube down his throat and suctioned out his lungs. They got a lot out. He also vomited then and they are concerned that something may have possibly gotten into his lungs and could cause infection over the next 24-48 hours. They took periodic x-rays

41

during the day to keep close watch. He also has a little air between his left lung and his chest wall, which they might have to release at some point with a needle and chest tube. By the time I left at 6pm, they said his lung issue was effectively resolved for the time being.

As if that weren't enough, as the day had progressed they became increasingly concerned about his heart. He was always stable, but only because they were keeping him there with lots of meds. His blood pressure was very low. His temperature was rising. So many teams of doctors were in and out of there so often: Transplant, Coronary, Critical Care, Neurology, even Nutrition. They kept hmmmm-ing with furrowed brows and hands on their chins, talking quietly among themselves and looking very grave. This scared the poop out of me. They told me exactly what was going on and said directly that this was potentially very serious. They said they would do tests to check the heart muscle. They tried to do a regular ultrasound of his heart, but they couldn't see it because of the ventilator. Next they anesthetized him again and accomplished it with a scope down his throat. The tests only took about 1 1/2 hours so I didn't have too much time to worry, but I did walk the halls at a fast pace while I called his kids. A doctor with a big smile came to get me. Jeff's heart itself is fine and strong. Now they can work like car mechanics to diagnose and treat each issue. They are back to adjusting meds and doing blood and urine cultures and everything else they do so well.

Jeff is going through an unbelievable ordeal in the very same way that he does everything else: he just puts one foot in front of the other and keeps going. His example gives me strength.

My niece and her family once again came to my rescue with almost no notice to feed the cats and fish while I hung out at HUP. What would I do without them?

So now I'm a little nervous wondering what today will bring besides Christy, who arrives in the early afternoon. She's taking the airport train to HUP to save me the trip. I've been very direct with her about how Jeff looks so she doesn't have a heart attack when she sees him. She insists she is prepared. I'm not so sure about that.

Every single person who comes into the room, even the cleaning staff, is so pleasant and kind to me. Even the doctors and nurses ask me if there is anything I need for myself. I couldn't possibly ask for more. Well, maybe just one thing...

xxoo M'ree
Organ Donors Save Lives

∞

3/15/2007   Still On Vent But Big Improvement

Jeff is still on the ventilator but things are clearly looking up. His night Nurse reported she was able to read his gestures without actually "talking". The sense is that he is now able to communicate with the staff. Her shift was over before I arrived so I don't have details to share, but I am so encouraged.

43

Everyone who comes in says Jeff looks totally different. He still has his issues, but each of them is resolving, some faster than others. His fever is gone. His feet and hands are less swollen. He is now responsive and aware, but not back to normal. As his sodium level drops, he should improve in that department. He liked having his glasses on. He is absolutely more peaceful. They keep checking everything and changing meds and ventilator settings. He got two bags of blood, plus albumin.

I hadn't mentioned this before, but all day yesterday I kept telling him that he needed to get better because Christy would arrive tomorrow. I'm absolutely positive that did it. He was clearly happy to see her and motioned for her to sit next to the bed so he could hold her hand. Then he promptly fell asleep and was zonked for the rest of the day. Christy didn't flinch and said that she expected him to look worse than he does. I'd much rather have that than the opposite.

The Critical Care Team (10 of them today) came by and went over every detail of his status. Everyone is very pleased at this point. The Transplant Team, the Neuro Team and the Respiratory Therapist each came separately later and all discussed what to do about the ventilator. They plan to do a tracheotomy (install a valve in the front of Jeff's neck, through which he can breathe) tomorrow; it would remain for "a period of weeks". With a tracheotomy, he will be off the ventilator most of the time but can go back on as needed, even if it's only providing some support. He will be able to talk, they will be able to suction his lungs whenever they want, and he can eat at least a little. They may or may not bronch him again first. The liver is still working perfectly. My thoughts went again to the donor and his or her family.

The Transplant Team Social Worker visited and talked to Christy and me for a while. They have so much to offer their patients, including weekly support group meetings and help with disability filings, etc.

TJ arrives tomorrow mid-day. It seems that Jeff is over the worst of it, at least for now. Please don't uncross anything yet.

xxoo M'ree
Organ Donors Save Lives

∞

3/16/2007   Good Day Today

This was a good day in all respects. First his condition. They didn't bronch him because he was doing fine without it. They did the tracheotomy at 7:30 this morning. When Christy and I arrived he was pretty sleepy from the anesthesia, but he looked pretty good. His blood pressure was not the best, but they expected that to improve as the anesthesia wore off, which it did. He's still out of it most of the time.

TJ had a not-fun time trying to get here. His plane was to land at 10:45. It did, but in Baltimore because of the snowstorm. He ended up on AMTRAK from there to here and arrived at 2:30pm. Jeff knew he was here.

The Transplant Team said the plan is to wean Jeff off the respirator over the upcoming days. Once he's off and stable for a couple of days, he will leave the SICU and go to the Transplant Floor. Then the next challenge will be to get some weight back on and strengthen him. They said that he is way, way behind in that respect, and definitely malnourished. He's still getting IV custom-mixed nutrition and also more high-test via the oral tube. He will not be able to eat until they remove the trach.

Very few other doctors came around, which proves that he's doing well. His overall condition continues to improve. I'm expecting he will be perked up more by tomorrow.

Christy and TJ and I went to the Chinese restaurant where Jeff and I often went. When the staff saw me without Jeff, they immediately asked where he was. They were sincerely concerned about how he's doing. They commented that his kids resemble him. When we got home, TJ shoveled and salted the driveway. Bless his heart.

This is more like it!

xxoo M'ree
Organ Donors Save Lives

∞

3/18/2007   Uneventful Redux

Actually, today wasn't totally uneventful. It's just that the weekends in a hospital are so much more low keyed than the weekdays. Jeff had a fever again, and again it was gone by the end of the day. He is very, very slowly being weaned off the ventilator. They adjust the settings lower for a while until he's working hard, then they set them back. It will go like that until he's able to breathe unsupported. His sodium is still high, but very, very slowly coming down. The skin tears on his arms are starting to heal and his Nurse changes the dressings every day. His Nurse adjusted his magic bed so that he was almost in a regular sitting position for a little while. It looks darned weird to see someone in his condition, with so much apparatus attached, sitting up rather than prone.

He was definitely more alert than before, even though that doesn't mean much response. It must be frustrating not to be able to talk, but he's not exhibiting that frustration yet. It actually seems to us that Jeff is on the road to recovery, even though it will surely be a long road. I can't wait to see him puttering around in our yard again.

I walked Christy to the airport train. Then TJ and I stayed for a while longer before we left for the day. TJ leaves tomorrow at around noon. Jeff's Nurse gave us the ok to come before visiting hours so TJ has time to say a proper goodbye.

The transplant miracle is just beginning to seem real.

xxoo M'ree
Organ Donors Save Lives

∞

3/19/2007   Up and Down Redux

Today Jeff has a fever again. The Critical Care Team is not
overly concerned, but they are doing cultures of everything possible
again so they can be absolutely sure that they are not missing any
bug. Because of the fever, he was not very responsive at all. I do
believe he knew that TJ and I were there. He didn't make positive
progress with breathing, most likely also because of the fever.

I probably didn't explain well, but a person with a trach tube
cannot speak unless/until they put a valve on it. After they take him
off the ventilator they will put in a valve. Sometime after that, they
will remove the trach. Also, he can't eat normally. After the surgery,
they had an NG (nasal-gastric) tube in for a day or two. Then they
changed it to an OG (oral-gastric) tube. They plan on keeping that in
until he can eat. If, for whatever reason, they decide the OG tube
isn't doing the trick, they will put in a G (gastric) tube, which would
be in his side going directly into his stomach. As of now, his
digestive system is doing fine with what he has.

We have a chemistry see-saw going on these days. His
sodium was a teeny bit higher today. His blood sugar is lower. They
keep adjusting his meds and other IVs so his body chemistry gets
into balance.

A doctor came in to put a few stitches into his liver incision, because it's been weeping a bit. There isn't any problem at all with the incision, but the stitches will keep it shut tight until it's totally healed. When I noticed that the doctor's coat said "DDS" instead of "MD", I asked him if he was a dentist. He had been a dentist but decided to go to medical school. He's going into facial plastic surgery, which makes sense because he was very skilled with the needle and thread.

TJ left at about noon. Both he and Christy are working on scheduling their next visits ASAP. I sure hope that he can interact with them more then.

It's very hard for me to sit there and watch him just treading water, not really here or there mentally. Today I actually decided to knit for a while, hoping that somehow he would realize it on some level and be comforted by it. I talk to him, but I can't tell if he understands what I'm saying. The hours and days just keep passing. I hope he doesn't remember all this.

xxoo M'ree
Organ Donors Save Lives

∞

3/20/2007   Spring Cleaning

It seems that the Teams (Transplant and Critical Care and Neuro) have decided that it's time for more aggressive action. Jeff's liver is fine. His kidney function is now normal. They have four priorities: his heart, lungs, nutrition and infection. For his heart, they are increasing his fluids, which should make the rhythm more consistent. As to the lungs, they are changing his ventilator settings more often to exercise him. He's doing ok, but he gets tired pretty quickly when he breathes on his own. They are keeping his lungs clear of secretions by periodic suctioning via his throat, which must not be pleasant, because Jeff reacts strongly each time. For nutrition, they are doing continuous feeds via the OG tube. They stopped the IV nutrition because they want his food to be processed by his digestive system. That is working fine, but they want to build him up faster. Since he has had a few fevers (none today, though) and since his mental status is not great, they are concerned about some underlying infection that they haven't found yet despite all their cultures. They sent an Infectious Disease Doctor in. She looked him over everywhere and paid special attention to his nose and mouth, using a high tech instrument called a flashlight. She reached no conclusions, but she did have Jeff's Nurse put an anti-fungal in his mouth for starters. It must have tasted yucky because he made quite the ugly face. She said she would return later with more team members.

Jeff's mental status is definitely not great; that is not easy to watch. He barely responds and is not very alert to anything. The MD/PhD head of the Transplant Team said that these issues could possibly be due to the specific immunosuppressant he's on now. He told me that they will do some tests, and said that within 24-48 hours we should have results and be seeing improvement. Besides that, they keep stressing that Jeff has been very sick for a very long time and was very low at transplant time. They said again that he will not recover quickly. They are being very cautious, but are absolutely positive about the long term outcome. That keeps me relatively sane.

Two Liver Transplant Team Social Workers came in to check on me. They are extremely nice, very helpful and very supportive. Jeff's kids are planning to come back in mid to late April.

If I had three wishes, the first would be for time to pass quickly for Jeff and the rest of us. Another would be for more hours in the day. The third would be for unlimited additional wishes.

xxoo M'ree
Organ Donors Save Lives

∞

3/21/2007   Testing Without Grades

Today Jeff was very much like yesterday: minimally responsive, except that by the end of the afternoon he started to move his legs a little. This seemed good to me. I say "seemed" because no doctor was there to comment on it. His Nurse liked it. Besides that, his vitals are good. His sodium level is still high, but that's ok for now.

When I arrived, the Critical Care Team was there doing their usual rounds. At the same time, other folks came to transport Jeff downstairs for a CAT scan of his head. The Critical Care Team decided to leave and said that they would come back later after they had the results from the CAT scan, but they hadn't returned by the time I left.

They also did an echocardiogram today. And they inserted a PICC line, which is a central IV line, installed in his upper arm. It's intended, as part of a normal progression, to replace the one in his neck. Then they did an x-ray to confirm that the PICC line is in the right place. Assuming that it is, the neck line comes out. Jeff's Nurse said that they have him scheduled for an MRI of his head, too, at the end of the day, but she hadn't confirmed that.

All this and I know nothing more than I did going in this morning. So you will just have to wait, too. Until tomorrow.

xxoo M'ree
Organ Donors Save Lives

∞

3/24/2007   He Loves Me!

At least, I think he mouthed the three little words. As well as a person can who has a G-tube taped to their face and dangling down inside the back of their throat. It was either that, or something I wouldn't want to type and send in an eMail. Anyway, you get the idea: he was much more awake and alert yesterday. He was also moving his legs and even lifted his left arm once. This is huge progress. He slept most of the time, but seemed very comfortable all day. His awful purple bruising everywhere is beginning to fade in places.

None of the usual big teams rounded yesterday while I was there. Plastics had been there earlier and said that his skin tears are doing ok from their perspective. Many of them are closing up. Jeff's Nurse continues to clean, dress and wrap both of his arms every day. The trach guys came in to change it, as they always do one week after insertion, to make sure it isn't clogged at all or harboring any germs anywhere. I left the room for that, even though they said I could stay. I didn't think I could handle watching. Oral Medicine came in and carefully examined the sore spot on the roof of his mouth that was probably caused by one of the early tubes. They said it is healing, but they took scrapings for pathology just to be safe. Also, another of the daily chest x-rays. Jeff's Nurse didn't mention whether ENT checked his ears, and I totally forgot to ask.

They lowered his ventilator setting again. The important concept to grasp is that the higher the setting, the more breathing support the ventilator is providing. He was down to 10 by the end of the day; I don't know where he started when they first intubated him, but while he was very out of it, he was generally above 15. If he's ever working too hard to breathe wherever they have it set, they set it higher. The ventilator is really extremely complex; there are so many aspects to just breathing.

Of course, he continues on the antibiotics, but he had no fever yesterday. And, oh, my goodness, he is so, so skinny. I'm almost used to seeing him in this state, but every once in a while when they change his gown I just cringe. With the high-test nutrition they are giving him, surely he will gain some weight just because he's lying there in the bed and not expending any energy.

The Social Worker stopped by to tell me about the 12th annual "Dash for Organ Donor Awareness", which will be on Sunday, April 22nd, at 11am - rain or shine. It's at the Art Museum, and there will be a 3k walk, a 5k run, and a 10k run. I'm going to sign up for the walk. If Christy and/or TJ are here, they can either walk with me or stay at HUP while I'm out.

People who have not been through this can't possibly have any concept of the enormity of the process. We all know that transplantation exists and that's about it. It's simple, right? You just go into the hospital and they put a piece of someone else into your body and you go home and get on with your life. Not.

xxoo M'ree
Organ Donors Save Lives

∞

3/25/2007   Like A Baby

Today was very uneventful, as you would hope for a Sunday. No doctors came in at all. Jeff has been stable since yesterday: no fever, no heart rhythm issues, and no ventilator issues. They lowered the setting to 8 around lunch time. We'll see how long it stays at that level.

He barely acknowledged that he knew I was there, then promptly went back to sleep. He stayed that way throughout the day, except for when his Nurses woke him for the usual things. I sat there, knitting, grateful to see him resting so totally peacefully.

Jeff's Nurse said that they plan to almost double his feedings, depending on how much he digests. Here's how they know: a certain time after a feeding, they hook up a huge syringe, about the size of a turkey baster, to the tube and suck out what is left in his stomach (it's called "residuals"). Then they just measure it and replace it. Is that bizarre?

Last night they put in a couple of additional stitches where they removed the last drain because it was leaking. No biggie to them.

When I talked with TJ, he said that he had a dream last night that the family came to our house to visit, and Jeff answered the door. I take that as an omen that he's really on the road back now.

On the drive home I felt absolutely giddy. Have you seen my favorite movie, A Christmas Carol? The original, I mean, with Alistair Sim. Anyway, I felt like Scrooge when he realizes that he's not really dead. Jeff has his liver; the worst is over. It's spring. It's daylight longer every day. Robins are at our feeders. A big, fat frog is swimming with the fish in the pond. The bulbs are coming up everywhere in our yard. Oh, yes, and the deer have decimated our rhododendrons. I could do without that.

xxoo M'ree
Organ Donors Save Lives

∞

3/26/2007   Almost Boring

Stable. Sleeping. Responsive to the same degree when he's awake. They had to up the vent setting to 13 overnight, but they put it at 8 in the morning and left it there. Oral Medicine came again to look at the roof of his mouth and it's healing well. They swabbed his nose to send more cultures. He is on very high calorie food and digesting it well. He's just recovering slowly and, we all hope, getting stronger by the day.

To look at Jeff, he still looks very sick. He IS very sick, which is why he's still in the SICU. He's no longer jaundiced, but his head and upper body are still covered with dark purple blotches. Both his arms are wrapped in gauze to cover his healing skin tears. Not that you can see them, but he has two raw areas the size of plums on his butt where his hip bones hit the bed. This is in spite of the "magic" bed that automatically inflates periodically on either side to keep his weight shifting. His hands, legs and feet are puffy one day, not the next. The trach strapped to his neck is more than a little gruesome, especially with the ventilator connected and puffing air into him regularly. Let's not forget about the tubes and bags connected to him, either. That he's so very extremely thin would shock anyone who hasn't seen him recently. He couldn't budge if someone yelled FIRE. The thought of him sitting up on his own is only a memory. It's just that because I have been with him through it all, I'm numb most of the time. Sometimes, though, it hits me like a huge wave and I am surprised that I'm still standing.

He's getting better now, though, despite all the challenges and setbacks. As the "Little Blessing" that friends mailed to him says, "Every breath is health". Breathe, Jeff, breathe!

xxoo M'ree
Organ Donors Save Lives

∞

3/27/2007   Almost Boring = Chronic

That explains it. Today I was chatting with Jeff's Nurse during a relatively quiet time. I remarked that he has been about the same for the past few days. She agreed but stressed that they are all very pleased with Jeff's status. She repeated what the doctors have been saying: that they are now concentrating on his nutrition and his breathing, building him up so he can breathe better and heal faster. You know how nurses aren't supposed to really tell you anything substantive because that's the doctors' space. She sort of stretched her space a little and said that Jeff has passed from the "acute" stage into the "chronic" stage. The initial issues have resolved and he's just slowly going about the process of healing. The other serious objective, of course, is to keep him from getting any other infections. She said that there are, indeed, some people who have a liver transplant and go home in two weeks, but said that those people were likely at home and relatively functional before the surgery. She also told me that as soon as they move Jeff to the Transplant Floor, they will begin serious rehab. So, anyway, that's why it is boring now. As soon as he can react and interact more and, of course, talk, things will be very different. She told me to get whatever rest I can now because I will need more strength later on. Oh. I see.

When I arrived today, he was sitting up, sort of, in "the pink chair". This is a funny looking contraption that is half hospital bed, half chair, built for sitting. Even though his bed-bed can be put into a sitting position, it wasn't designed for that purpose and so doesn't do it well. They put him in the pink chair for about two hours to exercise his heart and lungs. They timed it so he would be in the chair when I arrived; I didn't see what it took to get him there. They knew it would cheer me to see him sitting up. If I wasn't afraid he would murder me later, and if I'd had a camera, I would have snapped a shot. There sat my bag-of-bones husband, gorked, with all his tubes, etc., in his striped hospital gown, with the trach strapped to his face, his bony purple-blotched shoulders showing, wearing his blue plastic foam space boots. He was a real sight, I tell you. One reason why they only want the family in the SICU.

The rest is all the same. They turned the vent setting up overnight and only had it back to 9 by the time I left. I hope we don't have many more "chronic" messages before he graduates from the SICU. It's time for me to get some sleep.

xxoo M'ree
Organ Donors Save Lives

∞

3/28/2007   Is Less Boring a Good Thing?

Today Jeff was not as responsive to me as he has been. That's not so good. He barely opened his eyes and he didn't move his arms or legs, but he did wiggle his toes for me and his Nurses. On the other hand, he was down to a 7 on the vent by the time I left. This is very good.

The Transplant Team rounded. They are not seriously concerned, but there are two issues that need addressing. They did tell me again that Jeff's healing will not be a short process and it won't be straight line up, either. I hadn't mentioned this somewhat indelicate issue to you before, but today for the third day, Jeff has a bad case of the runs. They don't know exactly why. He has no fever. It could be the tube food. It could be the drugs he's on. Whatever. They are trying lots of adjustments to stop it, but it is continuing for the moment. This is not helping to achieve the nutrition target. To address this, they put in a new central line and they are now feeding him via IV plus the OG tube. This way, at least the IV nutrition will get to his body.

His low responsiveness could very well be due to the gastric issue. It could also be caused by one of the immuno-suppressant drugs he's on. You know how they always want to check every aspect as much as they can. So he has an 8pm date for a head MRI. Also, after I left, they were going to do another EEG. We will have results tomorrow.

This is a lesson to me not to get too comfortable. Ech.

I'd rather end on a light note. For each SICU patient, they have a fold-out chart (not to be confused with The Patient Chart, which is in a loose leaf binder) which they tape to the wall in the room. Each day, the doctors and nurses make notes on it as a quick reference document for whichever other doctors come in. Today they had to start a second monthly page for Jeff. This really discouraged me. I asked the doctor who started the second page what is the record for highest number of pages. He laughed out loud and said that two pages is nothing. They actually had someone in the SICU for over a year. I don't think I would survive that.

xxoo M'ree
Organ Donors Save Lives

∞

3/29/2007   Progress

Big thanks to each one of you who is praying so hard and sending positive energy to Jeff. It worked overnight. His digestive issue has magically cleared up. They don't know why, but who cares? When I arrived he was in the bed which was in a sitting position. He definitely knew I was there, even though he's not what you would call peppy. What a difference in one day. And, the vent was set to 5. That's FIVE, as in low.

He did have the EEG yesterday after I left, but his Nurse says it will take a couple of days to get that result. They never did the head MRI last night because the MRI department got behind. While I was there, Oral Medicine came to check out the sore spot on the roof of Jeff's mouth. It's healed, so they left and said they wouldn't be back.

They took him down for the MRI in mid-afternoon. Since it would be at least two hours until he came back up, I left. Here's the best part: his Nurse said that if he is stable when he gets back to the room, they intend to put him on the trach collar for an hour as a trial. This means that he will be breathing on his own. She said I could call at about 6pm (her shift ends at 7pm) and get an update. I'll do that, and I'll continue then...

6:15pm The MRI is done, but we won't have results until tomorrow. He's been on the trach collar for 1 1/2 hours, and is doing fine. They're about to take it off so he can rest overnight. Assuming all is well tomorrow, he'll be on it for a longer time.

You should see my smile!

xxoo M'ree
Organ Donors Save Lives

3/30/2007   Suspense

The MRI results were "inconclusive" according to his Nurse, who didn't have anything more to tell me. She said they will wait for the EEG results to evaluate it. I'd be happier if they said the MRI was negative, but I'll take this for now. No doctors came around while I was there today, so I didn't get to ask the question.

Jeff was in dreamland when I arrived. He had been back on the vent collar for an hour in the early morning and had gotten pretty exhausted. He stayed in dreamland all day except for a brief moment when he knew I was there. The vent was set to 10 to give him a rest.

His gastric issue has returned to a small degree. They still haven't figured it out, but the cultures were negative and he still has no fever.

Jeff's Nurse said that the skin tears on his arms and his butt are showing signs of healing. They said it will take a long time to heal. That's the common theme.

I know Jeff is not aware, but today is TJ's birthday. I told Jeff I had called TJ to sing Happy Birthday – our family tradition. It would have been just wonderful if the two of them could have talked, but that will have to wait. Maybe when TJ comes for his next visit, which should be in a few weeks. Christy is coming, too, but maybe not the same weekend.

Sometimes, because Jeff's mental status is so low, I wonder if he will come back to us 100%. I wish I could know what he understands or remembers. It must be such a nightmare for those with loved ones in comas; this can only be a teeny hint. I'm so grateful for what we do have.

Today during a quiet moment, I thumbed through a magazine named "Transplant Nursing" or something like that. There was an article about trying to revise the transplant system so that more organs are available and so that people don't have to get so sick before transplant. It said that over 7,000 people die every year while waiting. It made me realize what a miracle we have experienced.

xxoo M'ree
Organ Donors Save Lives

∞

3/31/2007   Breathing On His Own

When I walked in today, Jeff was on the trach collar, breathing regular oxygen on his own. I hadn't seen it before. It's no different from the vent, but the connection now goes to the oxygen in the wall vs to the ventilator. And the vent monitor screen is blank. It's freaky because I'm used to being able to watch it track his every breath. His color was very good but he did seem to be working hard. That's fine, because it's the exercise they intend for him. After he was on for an hour, they put him back on the vent, set at 10. He did know I was there and was moving his arms. That's more awake than he's been for a number of days. Then his Nurse and a helper bathed him and changed his linens and he went into a deep and comfortable sleep. The intent is to put him back on the collar for another hour this evening.

I'm sure I won't get the MRI/EEG results until Monday when HUP wakes up again.

I just sat and knitted until I gave myself permission to take the rest of the day off. I'm going to the movies, and then I'm taking a l-o-n-g bubble bath.

There was another startling statistic in "Transplant Nursing" that I forgot to tell you. At any given time, UNOS has about 90,000 people on transplant lists. And Jeff got a liver somehow. He must still have work to do on this earth. I'm starting a list for him.

xxoo M'ree
Organ Donors Save Lives

∞

4/1/2007   His Birthday Sunday

So it was a day of rest. The Respiratory Therapist said that he was tired from two days of trach collar trials and that he needed a day off. So no trach collar. The vent was set at 10. Nothing else happened all day. Amen.

I took a card that folded out to about 2 1/2 feet long and says "Happy Birthday" in huge red letters. I hung it on the bulletin board opposite his bed. He was awake enough to know that I told him we would have a party when he comes home. He put up his left hand as if to say, "no way". He's definitely in there, just not strong enough to be responsive. He was moving his legs and his left hand, but not his right for some reason.

His Nurse bought him a Happy Birthday balloon and had it floating from the floor next to the bulletin board. That was so sweet of her. I will share the other birthday and get well cards when he can appreciate them.

Tomorrow I expect to hear about the MRI/EEG. I'm anxious to learn the results.

xxoo M'ree
Organ Donors Save Lives

∞

4/2/2007   Weekday Progress

It's so obvious that the weekend is over; the SICU activity level is way, way up. The Critical Care Team rounded before I got there, as they often do.

When I arrived, Jeff was on the trach collar, very comfortably breathing oxygen on his own. They started him at 10:15 and didn't take him off until 2:45. That's just excellent. They won't put him back until tomorrow.

Then something new. They decided to switch his feeding tube from the OG (through the mouth) to a dobhoff. The dobhoff is a much smaller, more flexible tube that goes through the nose, through the stomach, and into the top of the intestine. It's more comfortable for the patient and it reduces the possibility of infection because it's not in the mouth and offers less chance for any aspiration of fluid. They insert it in stages. First they put it in as far as the windpipe. Then they x-ray it to be sure it's not headed into the lungs. Then they advance it into the stomach. Then they x-ray it again. Then they advance it out through the bottom end of the stomach into the intestine. Then they can remove the OG tube. They got it into his stomach by the time I left for the day. He didn't like the insertion, but he didn't cough or choke as you might imagine. I wouldn't like someone sticking a tube in my nose, either.

The Transplant Team scout arrived at noon to tell me that they would be rounding at 1pm. They never got there, so I don't know any more about the MRI/EEG from last week.

Jeff's mental status is a little improved. He's definitely in there. He absolutely knew I was there, but he's still minimally responsive. I think his neck is stiff, because he doesn't shake his head or nod like he did in the beginning. He was still moving his left arm but not his right. He moved both his legs. He responds to commands. He was somewhat more awake than the day before. His gastric issue is very, very mild. He had a little more edema today than yesterday, but that waxes and wanes. His skin tears are very slowly healing, but he has a new one on his neck under the strap that holds the trach in place and near the central line. They are taking special care with that one.

He's in the best hands he could possibly be in. I'm comforted by that.

xxoo M'ree
Organ Donors Save Lives

∞

4/3/2007   RIP Goldfish

Maybe it's because yesterday was full moon. Anyway, the day before when I went outside to feed the goldfish, all 11 of them were swimming around just as happily as you please. Yesterday, there were only four. I know that's right because I counted five times to be sure. When I would complain about the squirrels eating the bird seed we put out, Jeff would say that they are God's creatures, too, and they are entitled to eat. Well, I sure hope that I never identify the culprit, because I would not want to feel malice towards another of God's creatures. I must be closer to the edge than I realize, because I had a mini-meltdown right there in the yard. And now I wonder how many fish will be left when I go out this morning. You know, I figure that whatever took the others will come back for seconds. And I feel some level of guilt for having the fish in harm's way. No, that's not our fault, either, because the fish were there when we bought the house. It's just nature's way. But I don't have to like it.

So what does that have to do with Jeff? I'll tell you what I didn't tell you in the last message because I was not even able to process it until now. It's about meltdowns. Yesterday, after the dobhoff tube was inserted and his Nurse had left the room, a couple of tears ran down Jeff's cheek. It's the first time he's done that. I just held his hand and asked him if he was sick and tired. He responded by lifting his left arm, as if to say, "Leave me alone." It broke my heart. There he lies, totally incapable of doing anything for himself, including talking and moving. He's been a prisoner in that bed since February 16th. No wonder he's not responsive. He's frustrated and depressed. And he's probably mad as hell, too.

I'm going to bring this up to the Transplant Team today. Maybe the transplant psychiatrist can help Jeff, even in his current state. I'm also going to reschedule the appointment I had with the psychologist for the day Jeff ended up having his surgery. It's time for me to get some help for myself, too.

xxoo M'ree
Organ Donors Save Lives

∞

4/3/2007   Four Goldfish, One Frog, and Wow!

Fast facts first: as of this morning, we still have four goldfish and one frog. Maybe that fish dinner gave the culprit indigestion so he/she didn't return. Hooray!

Today our friend, Galen, donated his time to take me to HUP

and spend the day with me and Jeff. Galen and I made the deal that I would ask Jeff's Nurse if he could come into the room, then I would ask Jeff if it was ok with him. We would do whatever circumstances dictated.

When I walked in, the Neuro Team was in Jeff's room. He was very comfortably on the trach collar, with no OG tube. The Neuro people were smiling and talking to Jeff. He was awake and responding to them, including mouthing words, sort of. They told me that he had done everything they asked of him, and that they were very encouraged. Right away I asked them about the MRI/EEG. They said that the tests showed no seizures, no strokes, and no bleeds. They did find some changes deep in the base of the brain that are absolutely consistent with someone who has had wide fluid swings in their body for a long time, and that his status should continue to improve. Whew, what a relief!

They left and Jeff's Nurse said that absolutely Galen could come in. I asked Jeff if he would like to see Galen and he nodded (for the first time in many days) yes. So the two of us sat with Jeff and talked to him for the rest of the day, thank you Galen. He slept a lot, but when he was awake, he was more awake than he has been since just after the transplant. He was moving his left hand (still not his right) and both his legs. I asked Jeff if his neck was stiff and he nodded yes. I adjusted his head and he indicated that it was better.

The Respiratory Therapist came in and told us that the collar target today would be 6 hours, assuming that he was comfortable.

After a rest, tomorrow's target would be 12 hours. When he can do two 12-hour stretches comfortably, they will give up the vent, still watching carefully and checking blood gasses, of course. The Therapist said that Jeff was doing splendidly. He was still on the collar when we left for the day.

They are still working on his gastric issue, which is not very bad. They changed one of his antibiotics and also his tube food. They never give up.

Later one Critical Care Doctor came in and said that Jeff is 1 1/2 days ahead of their overall expectations for the week. This is really something, given how he has been recently. I'm so encouraged, but I'm also very aware that things wax and wane.

The Transplant Team intended to round, but again they never arrived, so I didn't get to talk to them about depression, etc. Before we left, I took Jeff's Nurse aside and told her in detail about my concern. She promised to discuss it with the Transplant Team. I asked her opinion about whether Jeff could have more visitors. She said at this point, absolutely yes. So that's the verdict, friends. He's in the Neuro-Surgical Intensive Care Unit ("SICU"). Visiting hours are 11am to 8pm. If you go on the weekend, you have to stop at the guard's desk, but when you tell them you are going to the SICU, they will say you don't need a pass (huh?). No sick people, no children. Two at a time maximum. There is a sink just outside the SICU door for hand washing. Then when you go into his room, there is a hand sanitizer dispenser on the wall at the door. Everyone is supposed to use it going in and out.

Tomorrow will be my first day not going to HUP, because I have to be at the Social Security office to apply for his disability benefits. Jeff will have the same Nurse tomorrow, and she knows I will call her.

I will sleep like a rock tonight, and that's a promise.

xxoo M'ree
Organ Donors Save Lives

∞

4/4/2007   Maybe I Should Stay Away More Often?

Today I didn't go to HUP because I had the pleasure of a command performance with the Social Security Administration to apply for Jeff's disability benefits. It really wasn't bad, just more-than-a-little bureaucratic. The good news is that since he's had a transplant, he's automatically eligible; no debate. Now that's done.

So I spoke with Jeff's Nurses twice today. The first thing is that he has been comfortable on the trach collar since 8am. The goal is 12 hours, so if he remains comfortable, they won't put the vent back until 8pm. The surprising thing is that at 9:30am, without advance warning, three people from Physical Therapy showed up. They asked Jeff if he wanted to sit up. He nodded yes, so with his Nurse watching, they had him sitting on the edge of the bed with his feet on the floor! His head was on his chest, and they asked him if he could hold it up. He did, for about 30 seconds. They were amazed, since he has the trach in and he's been virtually immobile for one month as of tomorrow. They said they would not come back until Friday. I can only imagine what he will do then.

We all know how stubborn he is. I guess his mind is finally made up.

xxoo M'ree
Organ Donors Save Lives

∞

4/5/2007   First Forth, Then Back

Last night was not the best. At some point he vomited (they don't know why), then may have aspirated some of it. They had to remove the dobhoff tube and suction his lungs. The ordeal exhausted him and set his mental status back. So today was another day of rest. Even though his vitals were fine and he was doing fine on the vent, they decided not to put him on the trach collar at all so as not to sap what little strength he has. His mental status was improving as I was there, but he was not back to the day before.

So they had to do the dobhoff insertion routine again, complete with two x-rays. He took it like a trooper.

To distract me, the Social Worker came to visit and took me on a tour of the Transplant Floor, where he will go next. Oh, my goodness, it's like the Taj Mahal. Fancy, big private rooms. Peace and quiet. Very plush furniture. He will appreciate it. They only have liver and kidney transplants and gastric bypass patients there.

The Social Worker and I also had lunch together. I took the opportunity to tell her about Jeff's crying episode. She promised to discuss it with the Transplant Team and said she's sure they can do something for him. I hope so.

Speaking of mental health, this morning was my appointment with the psychologist. I like her, too. After we talked for an hour, she said that she doesn't think I need regular visits, but I'm welcome to call her whenever I feel the need. She basically let me dump on her and validated what I've done and am still doing. I'll admit, it did feel good to just talk and cry. It's good to know I have an out if I think I might explode. I'm hoping those times are about over at this stage in the process.

xxoo M'ree
Organ Donors Save Lives

∞

4/6/2007   Not Quite Boring

A few little things today. Best first. Jeff greeted me with a mouthed kiss and "I love you". Oh, wow! It's been a long time coming and it felt so great.

He only did 1 1/2 hours on the trach collar and got tired, so no more until tomorrow.

While I was helping Jeff's Nurse change his gown, I saw that the staples have disappeared from his incision. It's covered with steri-strips. Nobody told me that it was done and I hadn't asked.

He vomited during the day, but it was not a serious event. Regardless, they will do an x-ray just to be sure nothing strange has happened. He has no fever and is not ill. It's always something.

Physical Therapy did not come by; I'm sure that's because of the prior bad night he had.

His vital signs are all good. He's definitely on the road to recovery.

The upcoming weekend will be quiet, as usual. I'm going prepared with a book and knitting.

xxoo M'ree
Organ Donors Save Lives

4/7/2007 Adjusting

He still loves me, or, he loves me again. That's good. He's pretty aware when he's awake.

He vomited again and they still can't figure out why. The x-ray was negative. Still no fever. So they are changing things to try and stop it. Different food, for one. Also, they inserted another OG tube so they can suction any air out as well as any offending fluids.

They did, and he said he felt better.

He's also puffed up with fluid everywhere he could possibly be, which has happened from time to time, but is more pronounced now. They don't understand that, either, but are adjusting drugs to help stop it.

His left foot is turning out, which is what the blue boots are supposed to help prevent. They will keep them on longer to stop that.

They did say that if he was stable throughout the day they would probably put him on the trach collar later, but that hadn't happened by the time I left.

I am anxious to see if any of the issues are improving by tomorrow. I'm sure that the Critical Care and Transplant Teams are watching closely, as usual, but neither of them was around during my visit.

Tomorrow after I leave HUP, I'm joining our friends, Anthony and Maria, for the traditional Italian Easter feast at their house, so don't be surprised if my update isn't published until Monday morning. I'm liable to be too stuffed and relaxed to log on.

xxoo M'ree
Organ Donors Save Lives

∞

4/8/2008   Awake

Today Jeff was more awake than he's ever been. He was watching the Masters golf tournament most of the day. Jeff's Nurse said that last night they turned off the TV, which he didn't want them to do, and turned out the lights to encourage him to sleep and get used to night and day again. I think it worked, at least somewhat. How much he comprehends may be another story. When Jeff's Nurse asked him what month it is, he mouthed: "June". Now, to be fair, I can't imagine how he would know what month it is given how long he's been there and what he's been through. I don't think he could have told them what month it was when he was admitted. No matter. He knows me and he understands what is going on. I asked him how he is feeling: he lifted the left side of his upper lip. Made me laugh.

Physically, he's making progress again. They put him on the vent collar at noon, and he was still on when I left at 4pm. No vomiting. He's still very bloated with fluid, but it's less than the day before.

We'll see what happens tomorrow when the weekend is over and the teams are back in force.

Easter dinner at Anthony and Maria's was like a vacation. The table was groaning with way too much food better than any restaurant I know. There were 14 very diverse people, and we laughed ourselves silly. Everyone is praying for Jeff's recovery.

The Dash for Organ Donor Awareness is now two weeks away. I've signed on to the Penn Transplant Team, which is second in fundraising at this moment. The heck with statistics; they are first in my book.

xxoo M'ree
Organ Donors Save Lives

∞

4/9/2007   Sitting Up, Sort Of

Jeff was on the trach collar when I arrived, with the bed in the sitting position. Pretty awake, but not as much or as long as on Sunday. He stayed on the collar comfortably for 4 1/2 hours. They took him off and planned to put him back on for another four hours after a two-hour rest.

Then Jeff's Nurse and a helper sat him up in bed. He had nothing to do with the effort, but they did keep him in that position for five minutes and he was stable. He was not able to hold his head up; he said his neck hurt. They called PT to have them do some work to loosen it and lessen any pain he may feel. He fell asleep as soon as they put him back down. It must be exhausting. You should see the nurses in action. I'm amazed at what they can do and with seemingly little effort on their part.

They put the dobhoff tube back in again. He still has the OG tube working as suction to keep his stomach calmer.

His red blotches are slowly fading. His skin tears are slowly healing. No vomiting, but he said his stomach was upset. They have been trying various things to lessen his discomfort. I asked him to hold his hand up when he needs anything so we could question him to figure out what it is. Now that he is fairly responsive, why should he want for anything at all? We may all regret what we wish for before this is over. Nah!

The Transplant Team scout said they were coming, but they didn't show again. Their emergencies make them late and then I miss them. I hope to see them again soon, because I love to see and hear their reactions. Clearly they are pushing him, gently, to progress now that he's more stable. This is so encouraging. He is so strong, even though he looks so very frail. I can't wait to have him back home.

xxoo M'ree
Organ Donors Save Lives

∞

4/11/2007   Bad News – Good News

First the bad, but it's not really bad. Jeff's urine tested positive for VRE (vancomycin-resistant enterococci). This is an infection common in hospitals, particularly in those who have had catheters for a long time. It's not even bad enough to require Jeff to take a separate antibiotic, but it's very easy to spread by touch. Standard hospital protocol when this occurs is to put the patient on "precautions" for the rest of their stay. "Precautions" means that whenever <u>anyone</u> goes into the room, even for a moment to pick up trash, they must wear both a gown and rubber gloves. Coats must stay outside the room. Handbags are permitted, but best not to have them. So that's the rule now. There is a big bin outside the door with new gowns and also boxes of gloves. You take them off inside the room before you leave. The gown goes into the "soiled linen" bin and the gloves go into the red waste bin. Then you use the hand sanitizer on your hands. You can imagine that knitting isn't exactly easy wearing rubber gloves, so that's probably the end of that pastime. The gowns are not glamorous and they are very hot.

Ok, that's it for the bad. There is lots of good. Jeff continues to show pretty dramatic improvement. The Transplant Team is very impressed and encouraged. The head of the Team told me yesterday that when we have both (not just either, he said) 36 consecutive hours off the vent and also three consecutive days of "less than critical" (however that is assessed) nursing care, Jeff will move to the Transplant Floor. Clearly it is in sight, but not just yet.

Jeff's Nurses will now sit him up every day. When PT comes around, they will also sit him up. Yesterday he held his head up while sitting. His vitals were also stable while sitting, particularly his breathing, which is excellent. He is getting much stronger.

They put him on the trach collar at 7:45am and he was still on it when I left at 4pm. They planned to leave him on for at least 8 hours, if he could tolerate that long.

His vitals are more stable more of the time. He is more awake and alert and communicative. When the head of the Transplant Team asked him how he was feeling, he gave the OK sign with his left hand. Everyone cheered out loud and I teared up.

I asked the Transplant Team if the Psychiatrist could visit Jeff, telling them about his crying incident. The Head thanked me for bringing it up and said it's an excellent idea. He gave the rest of the Team and students a little talk about needing to care for the whole patient. It was arranged before I left and will happen during my visit today. I'm very interested to see how he conducts the visit and learn what we will learn.

The nurses. I haven't talked about this before, but the nurses rotate their patient care duty and it's most common for Jeff to have a different nurse every day. Sometimes, a nurse will have him for two days running, depending on their schedule. He's had Sarah for a couple of days now. Yesterday, Sarah told me that she has elected to be his day "primary", which means that whenever she is on, Jeff will be hers. I didn't even know this, but he has a night "primary", Debbie, whom I've never met. Anyway, Sarah is about 5' tall and must weigh all of 100 pounds. She looks like Miss America and is absolutely, genuinely as sweet. I'm very happy with this arrangement.

We will surely have more bumps in the recovery road, but here's to more of these good news days!

xxoo M'ree
Organ Donors Save Lives

∞

4/11/2007   Less News

Not as much happened today as yesterday, but there is much progress.

Yesterday he ended up on the trach collar for 10 hours. Today the goal was/is 16 hours, if he can make it that long.

PT was there when I arrived and they had him in the bed in a sitting position doing leg and arm exercises, basically push/pull. The push is him working for strength building; the pull is the other person stretching his muscles. I'm charged with repeating them 10 times on each limb every hour (which I didn't do today because he was totally exhausted and slept the rest of the day). PT will come a couple of times a week for a start.

The PICC technician came to install another type of PICC line that will be able to be used both for IV TPN feeding and other injections. They x-rayed it to be sure it is in the right place. If it is, they will remove both the existing PICC line and the central line. That's one less potential infection site.

A Psychiatrist came to visit and got the whole history from me. We agreed that he's not depressed now, so she woke him to ask him directly if he was sad or depressed. He said no. So the plan is that they will keep a watch on him as he gets more communicative. She commented that it's clear I am proactive so she will assume that if I have anything to tell them, I will. She's right. She also told me that the improvement in his mental status coincided with their change in his immuno-suppressant drug. As we suspected.

The bad news for today is that by the time I left, he had a fever again. 101.something. Ech.

xxoo M'ree
Organ Donors Save Lives

∞

4/12/2007   Assortment

Lots of assorted stuff today.

Jeff's fever was down, but is still there. His mental status was not as awake as the day before, probably because of the fever; they are not at all concerned. My brother, Joe, was in Philly for another reason and visited for a while. Jeff recognized him, but there wasn't much interaction to speak of, unfortunately for all of us.

Turns out that on Wednesday, he made it for 12 hours on the trach collar. Today the goal is/was "as long as he can go".

Also turns out that the Psychiatrist from yesterday was only a scout. The Psychiatrist who saw Jeff alone and then the two of us together before the transplant came today with the Psychiatrist from yesterday and another doctor whom I assume was a resident or an intern. Anyway, they tried as much as possible to communicate with Jeff.

They asked him if he saw things that other people didn't see. No.

Does he hear things that other people don't hear? No.

What month is it? July. They were ok with that because July is a month, even if Jeff doesn't know which month it is now.

Is it day or night? Jeff looked towards the window. They were ok with that because at least he looked towards the outside. His window looks out onto a wall, but you can see whether it's light out there.

What surgery did he have? Puzzled look; couldn't answer. He sort-of put his hand near the incision.

Does he feel sad? No.

Is he glad to see visitors? Yes.

Is he hopeful that he will get better? Yes.

Jeff would try to mouth some words, as much as he could with the OG tube taped to his mouth, but nobody could tell what he was saying. They would look to me, hoping that I would understand, but I didn't. They tried to get him to write, thinking that maybe he could write what he wanted to say, but it was very hard for him to grip a pen both because of the edema, and also because his right arm is now much weaker than his left. He was able to make the letter O, but not a T or a J. They gave up on that. Net is that they said that tears or frustration or anger are fine. Not wanting to see visitors or feeling hopeless is not ok. He will not receive any meds now. Psychiatrists will come weekly going forward and I'm to tell them if there is anything that alerts me. Good enough, but oh, it will be so much better when Jeff can talk and we can learn what's in his head. I want to know that he's still Jeff.

The Transplant Team visited and said that all his systems are in good order. He still has a good deal of edema, but nobody is concerned about it. They said that now they want him out of the SICU as soon as he's able, because while the SICU is very good at getting the systems working properly, they are not very good at rehab therapy. They are very pleased overall.

Tomorrow TJ is arriving at around mid-day to stay until Sunday mid-day. I have to work in my local office all day, so I won't get to HUP until after that. TJ will be our eyes and ears.

xxoo M'ree
Organ Donors Save Lives

∞

4/14/2007   Eyes and Ears

This info from Friday comes from TJ and Jeff's Nurse, since I didn't arrive until late in the day so didn't have much opportunity to observe. TJ said he sees a big improvement from the last time they visited, which was when Jeff was still in the "low mental status" phase after the big nose bleed.

On Thursday, he made 12 hours on the trach collar. The goal was another 12 for Friday. If he made it, that's three days in a row at that level. Pretty darned good.

He still had a low-grade fever. His mental status was apparently better than Thursday, but still not up to earlier in the week. He had good conversation with TJ in between snoozes. I was relieved when TJ told me that many times he couldn't understand what Jeff mouthed either. Sometimes I feel guilty that I just can't get it.

His edema was worse below his waist, but better above. Jeff's Nurse had him in a sitting position for a while and fluid is subject to gravity. His Nurse said that when she did the PT exercises, he did a lot of the work, which is great.

Step by step he's coming around. Time for another quiet weekend with more progress.

xxoo M'ree
Organ Donors Save Lives

∞

4/14/2007   Restless

When TJ and I arrived this morning, Jeff had been on the trach collar for about two hours, but his breathing was fast and he was laboring hard. The past three days must have tired him. They put him back on the vent for a rest and took him off again at about 4pm. The goal was to keep him on for a total of 12 hours for the day, if possible.

He was still running the low-grade fever all day. No one is concerned.

During the day, Jeff was definitely awake and alert. It's hard to find the correct word for how he seemed to me, but if you pushed me, I'd say he was restless. He was moving his feet a lot and it seemed to TJ and me that maybe his legs were bothering him. It may have been that Jeff's Nurse (this was the first day she had him) had the leg jackets on a little tighter than he was used to. We never did figure that out. He was also moving his hands, especially the left, a good amount. Also, he said that his stomach was uncomfortable, but that he was not nauseous.

One of the Transplant Surgeons came around and said that Jeff is doing a good job recovering now.

More tomorrow. One week to the Dash. I'm hoping for no rain, but nothing will stop me.

xxoo M'ree
Organ Donors Save Lives

∞

4/15/2007   Yin and Yang

Jeff finally made 12 hours on the trach collar on Saturday and they targeted the same again today. This morning when TJ and I arrived, he was having a hard time with lung secretions. Since the oxygen for the trach collar is humidified, it always increases secretions relative to the vent. Jeff's Nurse had to suction him a lot and it clearly tired him out. They put him back on the vent for a two-hour rest and then back on the collar. Today's goal was also 12 hours.

His edema was markedly improved today in his arms, hands, legs and feet. He looks so much more comfortable without all that bloating.

Mentally, he is definitely aware. No question now: he's in there. At the same time, you couldn't call him either alert or peppy. He is moving his arms and legs and can even turn his head a little. I guess it comes down to the nutrition and the fact that he is physically very weak. Remember that the doctors keep saying this is the big challenge. He still has that stubborn low grade fever, too. He sleeps a lot of the time. He is very cooperative with the nurses, but when I asked him if he would like me to help him do his exercises, he very clearly mouthed, "Leave me alone." Jeff's Nurse assured me that they do them, so it's ok if he doesn't want me to do them, too. I can accept that.

To me, the single most frustrating aspect of Jeff's

communications, even when his words are clear, is that it's impossible to understand his emotions. I have no choice but to accept that, too.

Just seeing Jeff every single day in his condition is beyond surreal. If there is such a thing as a broken heart, mine is completely shattered. If I allow my own emotions to come to the surface, I will absolutely fall apart. I can't afford that luxury. Jeff needs me. Someone recently asked me how "my husband" is. I realized at that moment that I don't have a husband. I have a patient. They must have transplanted a nurse's brain into my head. Yet more acceptance.

TJ left at about 10:30 and despite a bumpy flight due to the nor'easter, did land in North Carolina roughly on time. I'm sure that Jeff would have been as happy as I if he had to stay another night. Christy will arrive next Saturday morning to stay until Monday afternoon. She will have alone time with Jeff while I walk the DASH.

So much for another low-keyed weekend.

xxoo M'ree
Organ Donors Save Lives

∞

4/16/2007   "Marked Improvement"

That's what the head of today's Transplant Team said. And

that's what I saw today, too. Jeff was on the trach collar again when I arrived. Also, he was moving his arms and flexing his fingers as if he was exercising them. At one point I thought he raised his hand because he wanted me to hold it, but he said no, he just wanted to move. He seemed more fully aware. He still sleeps a lot, but when he's awake, he's aware. He doesn't look so much like a terribly sick person any more. His color is good. There's no way to verify his actual weight by the built-in bed scale because there is so much daily fluid fluctuation, but his face looks less gaunt to me. TJ thought so, too, last weekend.

The Transplant Team is very satisfied with his liver function. So satisfied, in fact, that they are reducing a bunch of daily tests to twice a week. They said he will be "their next miracle". One patient went to rehab today and it looks as though Jeff will be the next to go.

He still has that low-grade fever. Infectious Disease is still trying to figure it out, but no-one is concerned, because he is not actually sick by any other measure.

His skin tears are steadily healing. I'm told that the two pressure ulcers on his butt have shrunken to the size of silver dollars and are looking much improved.

He did 14 hours on the trach collar yesterday. Today's goal is 16 hours. If he makes that, tomorrow's goal will be 24 hours. The Respiratory Therapist said that when he does 48 contiguous hours comfortably, they will remove the vent from the room and he will just remain on the collar until they put a valve in his trach. Humidification is the key. When you breathe through your nose, your nasal passages humidify the air. When you breathe through a trach, the nasal passages are bypassed, so there is no humidification. The trach collar supplies humidified oxygen. When your trach has a valve that you can close, you can breathe through your nose. Got that?

Nutrition remains the big hurdle, but they said that they are feeding him as much as he can physically tolerate, and that he's absorbing it well.

I was comfortable leaving a message for TJ that by the time he comes for his next visit, Jeff is likely to be in another place. Let's hope for that.

xxoo M'ree
Organ Donors Save Lives

∞

4/17/2007   Changed His Bed

Before I forget again, yesterday was the first day of a new wall chart. This one is number three.

Jeff's Nurse and two helpers had him sitting on the edge of the bed when I arrived; he was only able to lift his head a little. They kept him sitting for five minutes and said they would repeat it in the evening, then twice daily going forward. Since I walked into the room when he was already sitting and his gown was open, I saw his back in that position for the first time. It shocked me more than a little to see how extremely thin he is. His shoulders, shoulder blades and ribs are just under his skin. When he's lying in the bed, you get a false overall impression because of the remaining ascites and edema. I'm very glad that our mattress at home is a super-thick latex foam model with a pillow-top. It should be comfortable for him while he's gaining his weight back.

The fever is finally gone.

Our friend, Anarie, visited today for lunch and the afternoon. Jeff gave her a big hello smile. He really IS in there.

Just in case you might be wondering how Jeff could possibly change his bed, let me make myself perfectly clear and say that the nurses exchanged his bed for an even more high-tech one. It's called a Sports Bed; who knows why? Anyway, it looks just like the other bed, but it has two hydraulic features that the nurse programs for operation: it periodically (about every two minutes, maybe) inflates alternate sides of the bed to sort-of roll Jeff from side to side a little bit to help speed the healing of the pressure ulcers on his butt (they said this bed feels like being on a boat, which Jeff will enjoy); and it periodically percusses his back to loosen his lung secretions, then gently vibrates to make him more comfortable after the percussion. Jeff's Nurse stressed that percussion is never pleasant, regardless of whether a person or the bed does it. At any rate, all this both speeds Jeff's healing and saves the nurses work. They hadn't programmed the percussion by the time I left, so we didn't witness that, but the side to side rolling looked very comfortable to me and Anarie.

The morning sitting and bed changing exhausted him, so he slept most of the day. They left him on the vent for rest. They said they would decide later whether to put him on the trach collar.

So the mystery of the day is how (not to mention when) his dobhoff tube had gotten pulled almost all of the way out. I mean that the end was just in his nose instead of all the way down through his stomach and into the top of his intestine. We realized it when his liquid food started dripping out of his nose when Anarie and I were saying good bye. Jeff's Nurse was baffled; it's taped to his nose so how could more than a foot of it slip through the tape? You can bet they will be working hard to figure this out so that it doesn't happen again. Regardless, now they have to put it back in.

Didn't see even one team during the whole day.

xxoo M'ree
Organ Donors Save Lives

4/18/2007   Resting

Turns out that there was another chapter to the dobhoff tube issue from yesterday. There was concern that Jeff may have aspirated some of the food from the tube as it was coming out. You may remember that this happened a while back, as well. As a precautionary measure, they bronched him during the night, and they did find some bile in there so they put him on a prophylactic antibiotic. They won't reinsert the tube until tomorrow. The bronching process exhausted him, so they let him rest on the vent all day; he slept very soundly almost all the time. Also, they didn't make him sit up last evening or today. They did do his leg and arm exercises, but that was it.

His ascites is accumulating, so they will give him some diuretics to help lessen it. They are also getting heating pads to use for his stiff neck; PT is not able to address this in the SICU, for whatever reason.

I got to see the bed percuss him for 10 minutes, then do the 10-minute vibration. The percussion made a pretty loud, banging sound, like a toned-down version of a jackhammer, if you can imagine that. It must not have been too uncomfortable, though, because he slept right through it. It's going to do that every four hours.

The Transplant Team came around, this time headed by the Surgeon who performed Jeff's transplant. This is the first time I've seen her since just after the surgery, when she was still in her OR garb, exhausted from the long procedure. She is so tiny and gracious, with such a genuine smile. They are very happy with Jeff's recent progress. I asked her if the donor's family had been told that someone got the liver and was doing well. She said yes, and also offered to get me info from the Gift of Life organization, who will forward a letter for me. On the way home in the car, I was trying to gather my thoughts for that letter and found myself once again in tears thinking of their ordeal. This is a real life miracle.

xxoo M'ree
Organ Donors Save Lives

∞

4/19/2007   Partial Rest

Today was sort-of another resting day. I didn't see any teams. They had Jeff on the trach collar for about 4 hours very comfortably, and then they took him off with the intent of putting him back on later in the evening. They intended to sit him up during the evening, but not before that. They also decided not to try to reinsert the dobhoff tube until Monday. Meanwhile, he will continue to get the IV nutrition.

He has another very low grade fever.

He complained of having pain in his stomach as I was leaving. The staff always quickly responds to this complaint, given his surgery, so a Transplant Surgeon came right up and patted and poked him a bit. They did an x-ray to be sure that nothing serious was happening and promised to call me if there was anything I needed to know. No call, so I called them to check on the results. They concluded that he needed a laxative. That's surely the best thing it could have been. He should have an interesting night.

xxoo M'ree
Organ Donors Save Lives

∞

4/20/2007   Catching Up

This was a day of some physical progress. Jeff was back on
the ventilator for eight hours, very comfortably. Tomorrow the
target will be more. His fever is gone. He said that his stomach pain
is gone and that he's not nauseous, but his chest hurts. That was
because he was percussed for a while and had "a ton" of secretions to
be suctioned out. This is not only expected, but is actually good,
because he's doing very well with coughing, which is good exercise
for his lungs.

The Transplant Team rounded this afternoon, led again by
the Transplant Surgeon. They are all smiles now and said he's
making good progress, even if it's not a straight line up. Because of
the stomach pain from yesterday, they decided to do a CAT scan late
this afternoon, just to see what they could see. I'll be surprised if we
have results before Monday. I called just now, and Jeff's Nurse said
he tolerated it perfectly. They were just about to bathe him.

Having said all that, he seemed down in the dumps today,
which makes me very sad. When I arrived, he told me he was bored.
I guess we're now at the stage when he's well enough to know he's
not well and he's back to being sick and tired of being sick and tired.
Since he has no tube in his mouth now, he can mouth words. It's

very hard to understand him when he creates a sentence, though, so I asked him to do one word at a time. That helped, but there are still times when nobody can figure out what he wants to say. We tried the letter board, but his hands don't work well enough for him to point to the letters. Can you imagine how frustrating this is? We did understand when he told us that he does not like the space boots, but he must wear them to keep his ankles from rotating. The Social Worker picked right up on his mood and was telling him about her Golden Retriever puppy. He liked her stories and that distracted him a little. I also reminded him that Christy would be here by about lunch time tomorrow and he liked that.

When I left, I put ESPN on the TV so he could watch sports for the evening. And I just now thought of asking him if he would like me to read something to him. He likes that when we take long car trips; maybe it would be good now, too.

I'm looking for things to keep him mentally busy but not frustrate him further. It's not easy because my creativity seems to be on vacation.

xxoo M'ree
Organ Donors Save Lives

∞

4/21/2007   Grumpy?

What's that they say? Be careful what you wish for? Could it be that he's actually recovering?

I arrived to find him on the trach collar very comfortably, and wide awake. The Transplant Team rounded, led by one of the directors who has been with them often. He took one look at Jeff and said to him clearly - with a smile - "OK, you have no choice now. We want you out of this SICU. We want you to get off this ventilator so we can get you to the Transplant Floor where you can have serious rehab." He somehow knew that would pep up Jeff's spirits. It seemed to do the trick, because Jeff's mood improved immediately. They told me the CAT scan showed that everything is normal. He is carrying a lot of fluid, but that's not unusual. They are adding diuretics to help get rid of at least some of it.

Jeff's Nurse sat him up for five minutes and he was able to hold his head up for almost the whole time. Then he started fussing. He mouthed: FIX MY PILLOW. Done. Then he said he wanted the inflatable lower leg wraps off. Not done; they have to stay there to prevent clots. Big frown. Jeff's Nurse mentioned that he had already said he didn't want his space boots on, either. Here we go. I remember when, before the transplant so long ago, a nurse told me that I should rest because I would need my strength later.

Christy arrived, right on time. He was so glad to see her. He was distracted for a while. Then Christy took a drink from her water bottle and he asked for it. She and I exchanged looks and she told him he couldn't have it. He wasn't thrilled with that answer.

He was very awake for most of the day. When he finally started to fall pretty soundly asleep, Christy and I told him we were leaving. Jeff's Nurse said she wouldn't wake him to sit up again tonight.

I copied this text from a scroll hanging on the nurses' bulletin board in the SICU:

The True Meaning of Life

We are all visitors on this planet.

We are here for 90 or 100 years at the very most.

During that period, we must try to do something good, something useful, with our lives.

If you contribute to other people's happiness, you will find the true goal. The true meaning of life.

His Holiness, the 14th Dalai Lama

Dashing tomorrow.

xxoo M'ree
Organ Donors Save Lives

4/22/2007   Expletive Deleted

Jeff is really getting better fast now. How would I know if I was walking in the Dash today? Christy was with him alone for the morning and she told me. If she said it, I believe it.

After I got there, Jeff had been coughing for a while when his Nurse came in to suction him. Just at that moment, the Respiratory Therapist stuck his head into the room (he wasn't gowned and gloved so he couldn't go in) and said, "That's great, Jeff. Cough it up. Give us another big cough." Jeff looked at him through his coughing and raised one finger - I don't have to tell you which one. The Therapist, laughing, said he didn't want any more reverse peace signs. I did apologize to the Therapist later, stressing that Jeff's normal mode is not at all like that. He just brushed it off said it shows that Jeff is recovering and that he hasn't lost his spirit. Thank goodness he didn't take it seriously.

Yesterday he made 10 hours on the trach collar. Today the goal was 12-14. He sat up again and held his head up the whole time. Today he wanted ice, but he can't have it with the trach in because he might aspirate it.

Here is the sad part: Jeff's Nurse told us that last night he said he wanted her to call us to come back and take him home. He said he is still bored, but he didn't seem down in the dumps during the day. Everyone keeps telling him that as soon as he can get to the Transplant Floor, he won't be bored any more with all the physical therapy. We all know how stubborn and strong willed he is. He WILL do it now. He's had enough.

The Dash was just super. It was actually a little too hot (my car said it was 84 degrees) but it was a glorious day. I don't know the count, but there must have been at least a thousand runners and walkers. There was a rock band playing to liven it up. Lots of people had babies in strollers and there were many dogs along. There was a display of memorial quilts, with each block made in memory of a donor, some with photos, some with dates, etc. It was heart-rending. Many stories of both donors and recipients were told on people's t-shirts. One man's shirt had only a drawing of the upside-down incision line of a liver transplant, with a date below. I learned on the evening news that the first Dash was in memory of a man who died before they could find a liver. Maybe Jeff can walk with me next year.

xxoo M'ree
Organ Donors Save Lives

∞

4/23/2007   So Sad

Physically, Jeff is slowly but surely healing. He did almost 12 hours on the trach collar yesterday. They will advance him as quickly as he can handle it. The Transplant Team rounded and said his systems are very stable now. As soon as he is off the vent, he will leave the SICU. They decided to hold off on inserting any feeding tube because his stomach is still putting out a lot of bile via the NG tube. They would rather not put food in there until his stomach has calmed down. He's still getting all the nutrition he can possibly absorb via the IV. That is ok.

He got a fever again. He complained of leg cramps. He

wanted the space boots and the leg wraps off. We hate telling him "no" as much as he hates hearing it. He asked us a couple of times to take him home. I asked Jeff's Nurse if they had any medicine for homesickness. Everyone has difficulty reading what he mouths, even when we ask him to go one word at a time. His hand won't work well enough to write or even to point to letters on the board. He's totally incapacitated and he's absolutely miserable.

When Christy was ready to leave, she started to tear up. Then he started to cry. I tried my best not to cry, too; I just cannot fall apart. We tried to comfort him by saying that he was getting better and he just shook his head. We got him calm enough so I could take her to the airport train.

At Christy's suggestion, I sent an eMail to the Psychiatrist. He will be quick to respond. I really believe that as soon as Jeff can get off the trach collar and move to the Transplant Floor, he will be encouraged enough to be more positive.

Let's all pray for him to get the emotional and physical strength he will need to recover from here.

xxoo M'ree
Organ Donors Save Lives

∞

4/24/2007   Turnabout

It's happened before and I guess it will happen again before this is all over. My personal goal was to cheer him up in whatever way I could. There wasn't much to do in that department.

Jeff's outlook was very much improved vs yesterday. I didn't see any depression. His fever was down, then up again, but not high. He was sleepy, but alert when he was awake. He asked me to get into bed with him to watch TV. I tried my best not to appear too surprised by that request. I told him that his Nurse would be angry with me if I got into the bed (not that I could fit anyway), and he accepted that. Then, when I was going to the cafeteria for lunch, he asked me to bring him apple juice. I explained that he couldn't have it while he had the trach in because he would aspirate it, but that as soon as he could get off the vent, they would put a valve in the trach and then he could not only drink, but talk, too. He liked that. And I was really happy to hear that he has a yen to drink something that tastes good. That's impressive while on IV feeding, because most people are absolutely not hungry or thirsty. I also kept telling him how well he was doing physically. I told him, too, that all the daffodil bulbs we planted are coming up and starting to bloom. I said that I would take photos so he could see them.

He did 15 hours on the trach collar yesterday; that's the record so far. Today's goal is 16. And he only needed suction twice during the whole day up until when I left. That's super, because it means that his body is starting to deal with the normal secretions we all have without even realizing it. That equates to less critical nursing care, one of the criteria for moving him to the Transplant Floor.

The Psychiatrist sent word that he would come tomorrow.

All of our prayers are being answered and I am so grateful... but I know we'll need even more so please don't stop. We may be able to see the edge of the woods, but we're not out yet.

xxoo M'ree
Organ Donors Save Lives

∞

4/25/2007   Almost Back to Boring

Jeff was very stable all day, but he was tired and slept almost all the time. When he was awake, he was alert. He didn't display any frustration, depression, or anything else negative. His Nurses did sit him up, but he only made about three minutes (with them supporting him) until he was too tired.

He did have another episode of fast heartbeat overnight, which they stabilized by giving him meds. I asked Jeff's Nurse why it happens and she said that Jeff seems to be very sensitive to his electrolyte balance. Since they are giving him diuretics to reduce his fluid, his electrolytes are affected. They gave him potassium, too, but the balance is very delicate. The good news is that it's not a serious issue.

He made 16 hours on the trach collar yesterday: another record. They were shooting for another 16 today. If he does well, tomorrow the goal will be 24. Remember that Transplant Team

Head said after 36 hours straight, and also three days of "less critical nursing care", he can move to the Transplant Floor. I can almost taste it. I keep telling Jeff that he's doing really well and that soon he will be off the vent.

Christy wrote him a two-page eMail message. He enjoyed having me read it and paid strict attention the whole time.

The Psychiatrist hadn't arrived by the time I left.

The whole day was very peaceful and quiet. May there be more like this. The more of these, the closer we are to being home again.

xxoo M'ree
Organ Donors Save Lives

∞

4/26/2007   "Talking Trach" On the Way

Sixteen hours on the trach collar yesterday. Headed for 24 big ones today. It remains to be seen how soon he will get to 36 consecutive hours, which is part of the criteria for moving to the Transplant Floor. He's taken steps back before. I remember this saying: "Blessed are the flexible, for they shall not be bent out of shape." When he's absolutely ready to move, they will move him. And not before. Which is exactly what we all want.

Jeff's night Nurse said that Jeff was awake every minute overnight. The staff will try to get him back onto our day/night rotation right away. They did sit him up before I arrived and said he did fine. Anyway, he slept most of the day away. When he was awake, he was calm and not at all depressed.

Speaking of depression, the Psychiatrist did get there after I left yesterday. I haven't heard what transpired yet, but surely he intervened as much as he could. One of Jeff's Nurses made it a point to get me aside and tell me they are all taking every opportunity to encourage him and keep him cheery. Also, she said that she was going to try to get him a "talking trach" since he is doing so well on the trach collar. They can turn the valve from time to time to let him talk, depending on how well he tolerates breathing air. She said that they can probably get it by the weekend. That would be so wonderful for him because it would help to eliminate the huge communication frustration.

It seems that his SICU days are finally coming to an end. I have everything crossed for him and I know you do, too.

xxoo M'ree
Organ Donors Save Lives

∞

4/27/2007   Let's Cheer Him On

Oh, how I regret not being able to be at HUP for this particular day; I needed to work in my local office. I spoke with Jeff's Nurse at about 9am and again at 5:30pm. He started the day with a low grade fever but now it's down. But here is the real breaking news: at 7:30pm he will have been on the trach collar for 36 hours straight. His vitals are all stable. She asked him a couple of times if he wanted to go back on the vent and he said NO. Go, Jeff, go!

I can't wait to get there tomorrow morning. I'm going as early as I can get it together, partly because of the expected horrendous Penn Relays traffic but mostly because I just want to see his face.

xxoo M'ree
Organ Donors Save Lives

∞

4/28/2007   Sleeping Beauty

Well, he made it to 34 hours before they took him off the trach collar. That was just after I called in the afternoon. Today when I arrived he was resting on the vent. He was also sleeping, which he did the entire time I visited, except for a few brief moments. They did put him back on the trach collar at noon, but said they would check him every four hours and take him off whenever he gets tired.

The Critical Care Team rounded and said that they want to give him a little resting time before they go for 48 hours on the trach collar. They feel it does no good to exhaust him. One of the Transplant Team Surgeons visited and ordered some blood since his hemoglobin was down. They did a routine chest x-ray. Other than that, nothing happened.

What a peaceful weekend day.

xxoo M'ree
Organ Donors Save Lives

∞

4/29/2007   Sleeping Groucho

Not exactly sleeping beauty today. He was very
annoyed because I wouldn't remove his space boots when his Nurse
wasn't there. He said that I could do it if I wanted to. That's like, "If
Mom says, "no", ask Dad." I told him that I don't like saying no to
something he wants, but that it was the doctor's orders because if he
doesn't keep them on, he will have foot and ankle problems, which is
true. If I remove them, it may feel better now but it will hurt him
later. I gave him a big pep talk and tried to cheer him up. I guess it
worked to some degree because he asked for my hand and then he
kissed it. He hadn't done that before. I so badly want him to get off
the vent so he can move to the Transplant Floor.

To that end, he was on the trach collar for 10 hours
yesterday. They put him on again at noon and will let him go until
he's tired. They mostly leave it up to him now. While Jeff was
listening, the Respiratory Therapist told me that Jeff said he wanted
to go home. He said that he told Jeff that being on the trach collar
was the way to get there. I know he's very discouraged and
impatient, but I do think he understands that it's just a matter of time

now.

Yesterday my friend, Lindy, visited me for dinner and brought me a "Team of Angels". The Team of Angels is a golden pin with three angels holding hands, which comes with a poem to help the recipient through an ordeal (there are a number of them, customized to various circumstances). I read the information to Jeff and he became very emotional. I told him that we are not alone. I have it hanging on his bulletin board. If anyone takes it, I'll assume they must need it more than he does.

Maybe we will hear about the talking trach tomorrow.

xxoo M'ree
Organ Donors Save Lives

4/30/2007   Spelling

The Team of Angels is already hard at work. Jeff surprised me with a new skill today: spelling. This is huge, because now he can communicate. He said he wanted to write, but couldn't hold the pen or control his hand enough to make it legible. Then he asked for the letter board: a sheet of paper with the alphabet on it. Would you believe he was able to point to the letters and spell words? And what was his first sentence? "PANTS ARE ON TABLE NEXT TO BED." [He surely meant his bedside table at home, where he often leaves his pants at night.] Is that the best he could do? I was secretly hoping for, maybe, something like "I love you", but no. Since he's been so focused on going home, I interpreted this to be telling me what he wants me to bring to wear for the trip home. Then we were interrupted by his Nurse coming in to turn him to the other side. His second sentence? "I SLEEP BEST FACING THE WINDOW." The bad news is that she *had* to turn him the other way that time. He couldn't win. Nevertheless, he slept the rest of the time I was there.

As of noon today, he had done another 24 hours on the trach collar, and he was still chugging away when I left. They intended to let him go until he said he was tired.

Time for a skin update. He has only one bandaged tear, about the size of a 50 cent piece, remaining on his arm, but it is healing nicely. The others are dried up. There are three pressure ulcers on his butt, where his hip bones hit the bed. They are still open, but also healing nicely. They take the longest because he's always on them, which is why they keep turning him from side to side. His purple marks are all fading. Except for being so very skinny and also bloated, he looks healthy now. The overall improvement is tremendous.

I didn't see any teams today. Maybe tomorrow.

xxoo M'ree
Organ Donors Save Lives

∞

5/1/2007   Boris from the KGB

The Team of Angels is working non-stop. Today they sent us
Boris, who arrived just after I did. He said he was from the
KGB, but he was really from Physical Therapy. He's a bald Russian
weight-lifter type with a heavy accent and a big smile. He brought a
student with him for help. Together they exercised Jeff's hands,
arms, feet and legs, and sat him up on the edge of the bed.
They even tried to get him to stand up, but he couldn't quite do it.
I'm thinking that he didn't have the strength because he had already
been sitting in the Pink Chair and had a bath. Anyway, Boris said
that Jeff is still very strong. Boris had him smiling broadly at his bad
jokes; he would have laughed if he hadn't had the trach in. I believe
the whole session was very encouraging for Jeff.

I don't know exactly how long he had been on the trach
collar yesterday, because he had a new Nurse who wasn't able to
decipher the notes in the chart. He was on for at least 27 hours that I
can personally attest to. They did rest him on the vent for some time
overnight and put him back on the collar at 7:30am today. He had
no fever.

Jeff continued to spell all day. Sometimes he gets visibly
confused and stops in mid-sentence, clearly frustrated. Sometimes
he can do long sentences. He wanted to know when he would move
to "the other room". I gave him the straight story: as soon as he is
able to do 72 hours on the trach collar, they will move him. I told
him he was very close. He liked that. He hates the space boots

because they make his feet sweaty. He also spelled a sentence that made me think he is at least partly goofus. He told me to go into [name deleted]'s (a woman who used to work with him) room. I said that she wasn't at HUP. He gave me a look as if to say, "Oh, yeah."

I read him another eMail that Christy sent and his nose and eyes got red when she said that she missed talking to him. He loves to hear from Christy and TJ.

Today's mystery is that there were two balloons in his room. One was a smiley face and the other said Get Well. I asked him if anyone visited last night and he said no. I asked his Nurse and she didn't know who brought them. I will keep checking until I know who to thank.

No teams rounded while I was there. Tomorrow I won't be there at all because I need to be in my local office again. I'll call in and report whatever I learn.

xxoo M'ree
Organ Donors Save Lives

∞

5/2/2007   Whisper Down the Valley

Since I didn't get to HUP today, I can only repeat what Jeff's Nurse told me. It's not very colorful, but it's good news.

They put Jeff back on the trach collar at 8am today and they are going for 48 hours if he doesn't tire out sooner. He's comfortable as of now.

PT came today (but not Boris) to do exercises and sit him up. He tolerated it well.

His Nurse said he has been "trying to spell". I think maybe she doesn't have the time to be as patient as I do. I wouldn't have used the T word to describe his efforts. He was better than that for me.

He has not had a fever all day.

That's all the news that's fit to print.

xxoo M'ree
Organ Donors Save Lives

∞

5/3/2007   Whisper Down the Valley, P.S.

That was not quite all the news, it seems. Jeff's friend, John, called me later to say that he visited Jeff for a long while in the evening. Sounds as if they had a touching reunion. They talked in whatever ways they could. John read to him from a coaching (as in horse carriage driving) book. They just passed the time together.

During that visit, an amusing thing happened when the Transplant Team rounded very late. From John's description, we concluded that Transplant Team Head was leading them. John queried that the new liver is working perfectly, right? Yes, it absolutely is. Well, since that's the case, when Jeff is out of here, we can sit down together for a whiskey, right? The Transplant Team Head laughed and said that no one had ever asked him that question before. I have to observe that this series of questions would naturally come from an attorney's mind.

John said he told Jeff very clearly that he's going to make it. I'm sure that made a deep impression on Jeff's consciousness. It's one thing for me and the doctors and nurses to tell him, but this is something else. I'll bet he believes it now.

xxoo M'ree
Organ Donors Save Lives

∞

5/3/2007   Spa Day

Today Jeff was sitting in the Pink Chair to greet me. He wasn't happy because he said his butt hurt (remember the pressure ulcers, besides the fact that he is skin and bones). They put him back into the bed before too long. They also came up with a blow-up chair pad that they can use from now on to make it easier for him.

He said that he was happy to see John. It made him teary to think about it. He cried again when I read him Christy's eMail, but not as if he was depressed, just sick and tired. He so wants to be out of there. He indicated that he was not happy with his fingernails. The nurses aren't allowed to cut or file them, so it hasn't been done since before he was first admitted on February 16th. Needless to say, they were overgrown. I asked Jeff's Nurse if I could do it and she said yes. So I went ahead and filed his finger and toenails. It made him so happy. It made me happy, too. If he's concerned with his grooming, he's definitely much better.

He also had a visit from the Social Worker. She brought him a photo of her 10-month old platinum blonde Golden Retriever. It's now on his bulletin board. What a gorgeous dog! Jeff smiled a really big smile. He loved hearing about the pup's antics.

Everyone who comes in makes a fuss over him and tells him how much better he is doing and how much better he looks and that he will soon be on the Transplant Floor. I'm sure it all helps.

He remains on the trach collar, working towards 48 hours, which will be up at 7:30 tomorrow morning. We'll see what they do next.

Spelling continues in earnest. When I was leaving for the day, he asked me if I wanted to drive to Little Rock. I said maybe someday. He said, no, today. I said I didn't think that would work since I had to go home to do some more work. That satisfied him. I wonder where he thinks he is...

xxoo M'ree
Organ Donors Save Lives

5/4/2007   Che Garne?

For those of you who have never been to Nepal, "che garne" [pronounced "kay gar-NAY"] means "What to do?" It's a very common saying there. It applies in Jeff's room big time now.

Jeff is doing very well, physically, and is making steady progress. He can now turn his head from side to side, raise his head off the pillow, elevate his arms pretty high from his shoulders, and lift his feet off the bed.

The original two hurdles still remain, although they are much lower now. First, breathing. He didn't quite make 36 hours on the trach collar yesterday, but he's definitely closing in on 72 hours. They don't want anything to set him back in that department, so they are being justly cautious. Second, nutrition. He's doing very well on the IV food, but he has had nothing in his stomach since the dobhoff tube came out for the second time. They haven't tried that again because if it comes out again and he aspirates again, it's a big setback again. They know he's impatient to get out of the SICU, so they are very sensitive to avoiding setbacks. A complicating factor is that his stomach is often upset and is continually putting out a large quantity of bile via the NG tube. They have kept that in to prevent vomiting. They don't know why this is happening; it could be the result of some of his meds, though from the beginning they have been giving him something to quell it. It is important, though, to be sure his digestive system is working. Now they are talking about possibly inserting a feeding tube in his side so they can both put food in and take bile out. I'm not 100% clear on how this works. I'll learn more as their discussions formulate an approach. I'm prepared not to hear any more about this until Monday.

Psychologically is another situation altogether. He's mad as heck. He's frustrated. He's impatient. The good thing is that he's not depressed now, as far as I can tell. The first thing he spelled for me today was "F--- 'em". I tried not to show my shock and asked him what was wrong. He couldn't even give me an answer. He's just plain sick and tired. The Transplant Team rounded. Jeff's Nurse prepped them before they came into the room. The Lead very clearly told Jeff what great progress he has made and how close he is to moving to the Transplant Floor. Jeff spelled "TRACH OUT". The Transplant Team Lead said that in conscience they couldn't do that until they are positive he is ready to be taken off the vent, because a setback caused by that would be a big one. He said that he would ask the Psychiatrist to visit again. Maybe it's time for chemical intervention.

After that episode, Jeff's attitude improved a lot for the rest of the day. He asked me for a comb: another positive sign. He spelled out wondering how he would be able to get into our bed at home. It's a very thick latex foam mattress on a very tall wooden box instead of a box spring; it's about waist high to me. I told him that our friend, Anthony, had already volunteered to build us a lower box. Jeff asked me if I thought it would work to just replace the box with a board. That would be fine. You can see that he's thinking positively and imagining how it will be to come home.

One by one, these issues will all resolve. The Team of Angels told me so.

xxoo M'ree
Organ Donors Save Lives

∞

5/5/2007   Goodbye and Good Luck to the Vent

It's been a long time leaving. At 11am today, without prior announcement or ceremony, the Respiratory Therapist came into the room, unplugged the ventilator and wheeled it out of the room; she said he had been on the trach collar for way over 48 hours. Today is exactly two months since the transplant. Now they have him on the minimum oxygen setting for the trach collar. I said to Jeff, "Hey, there goes the vent. It's gone now." No reaction whatsoever. Can you believe that big brat? I was certainly not about to verbalize anything with Jeff listening and I knew it was useless to ask his Nurse, but of course the next step is to move him to the Transplant Floor. I have no idea when that will happen.

Also, as I was walking into the SICU today, there stood the Gastroenterologist who had acted as Jeff's PCP for years before the transplant. He came for a social visit with Jeff and was making notes in his chart. We talked for a while. Well, he was almost giggling with excitement. He said that we had come as close as it comes with Jeff's illness. Really, really close, he said. He is just thrilled with Jeff's

117

progress. He was talking about his color and his muscle strength, etc. He also said that it's amazing how far he has come in only two months. He said that he came all the way back from...from...he stopped without saying "the dead", but that's what he meant. He told Jeff that he wouldn't be on the [horse] coach at Devon [the major horse show] this year, but certainly next year. Also, it turns out that he was in the room when Jeff's friend John asked the Transplant Lead about having a whiskey with him later. He said that absolutely Jeff could have a whiskey now that he has a perfect liver. He just loves Jeff and Jeff feels the same about him.

I'm so happy and I'm thankful too for all the prayers and good energy. He's getting well!

xxoo M'ree
Organ Donors Save Lives

∞

5/6/2007   Might Move Monday

I didn't tell Jeff, because I don't want him to go into the deep pit if it doesn't happen for any reason, but his Nurse told me today that the tentative plan is to move him to the Transplant Floor tomorrow. I'm holding my breath, figuratively, while staying mentally prepared just in case tomorrow is not the day.

They removed his catheter early this morning. That's good, because it's just one more source of possible infections. He does remember how to pee after all this time.

He was grumpy today and he said his stomach was still upset, but he asked me to help him with his leg and arm exercises. He did more repeats than he's supposed to. He's unbelievably strong. He also asked me for his blue jeans. I told him that I took all of his clothes home when he had his surgery, washed everything and left it home.

He won't be able to talk until they give him a "talking trach". He will still be on "precautions", so visitors will have to don a gown and gloves. Visiting hours are daily 11am to 8pm. I know that they will be doing a lot of PT both in his room and in the gym while he's there and I don't know the schedule yet, if a schedule even exists.

Go, Team of Angels! When Jeff moves, I will leave the Team with the person in the room next door. He looks to be in his late teens and had some sort of head injury. He's in a coma. His parents are calm, but look very worried. People come out of his room crying. He needs the Team of Angels more than Jeff does now.

xxoo M'ree
Organ Donors Save Lives

∞

5/7/2007   Fait Accompli

Finally, 63 long days after his transplant, he's been moved out of the SICU to the Transplant Floor. Jeff took it as a non-event. His Nurses and the Respiratory Therapist cried and hugged me and I cried, too. This is such an enormous step, and it has taken so long to get to this point. While the transport people were installing him in the room, I went to get a snack and came across the one of the Transplant Surgeons in the hall. She, of course, knew all about the move, and was grinning widely about it.

The whole afternoon was taken up with his new Nurses getting him settled and getting to know him. He's spelling for them. They are already making him externally suction his own lung secretions and his own mouth. PT will start in earnest tomorrow. They warned him that he will be tired every day.

The Social Worker came by and did a dance in the room to celebrate. She's already checking with Bryn Mawr Rehab Hospital ("BMR") about the possibility of that being the next stop. They have a stellar reputation and it wouldn't be nearly as tough a commute for me as getting in and out of town every day.

Here's a quick update on his status:

He is awake and alert, and knows everyone. He is a little confused in some respects. This is normal for someone who has had serious liver disease. Remember the hepatic encephalopathy?

His new liver is working perfectly, as are all his other systems. No sign of rejection.

He is off the ventilator, but still has a trach. He is breathing oxygen on his own via the trach collar.

He won't be able to talk until they put a valve on the trach, which may happen very soon. He's spelling via a letter sheet. This is very frustrating to everyone.

His nutrition is still via IV. He won't be able to eat until the valve is on the trach. He is extremely thin.

He cannot sit, stand, or do anything else physical by himself. He can turn his head and raise his legs and arms off the bed.

Serious PT will begin tomorrow.

He has been given a phone, but he can't talk yet. The good news is that I can keep my cell phone on while in the room.

Visiting hours will remain 11am to 8pm. Most PT happens during the day, but the hours vary from day to day so there is no telling when he will be working. Everyone has to wear a gown and rubber gloves to enter the room.

I was all set to give the Team of Angels to the mother of the young man next door in the SICU, but he was not in the room for some reason and his parents were not there. I left them with Jeff's Nurse to pass them along from us. I'm sure if a miracle is possible for him, they will help it along. I'm praying.

xxoo M'ree
Organ Donors Save Lives

∞

5/8/2007   Would You Believe Standing Up?

There is no news about either the talking trach or the feeding situation. As with everything else, the staff will make the decisions as a team and will do what is called for at the proper time. I've learned that lesson. I didn't see any doctors today and didn't bother to ask his Nurse.

Jeff's Nurse told me that he had cried earlier in the morning because I wasn't there. They assured him that I was on the way. I do believe he's homesick, along with everything else he's feeling. I just try to be as cheery as possible every minute I'm with him.

The goal today was for PT to get a handle on exactly what Jeff is currently capable of doing, and to start work in earnest. When I arrived, they were already in his room. By "they", I mean three of them. They were so positive and encouraging. It's very clear that they will not let him off any hooks and that they have no time for self-pity; it's all about action. They tried a bunch of movements and pronounced his legs remarkably strong given that he's been flat on his back for so long. They said that they had originally intended to sit him in his reclining chair, but because of his leg strength, they said he should just stand up. He started to cry and said he couldn't do it. They insisted that he could and that they were able to support him. Believe me, I held my breath. They put the space boots on him, because they have hard, flat bottoms and straps around his ankles. With one standing behind and one standing in front, plus one spotting, they actually stood him up, not just once, but three times.

Now, he wasn't totally straight, and he wasn't standing on his own, and he didn't stand for more than a moment each time, but he stood on his feet. It was obvious that he was both shocked and thrilled. They said they will be back every weekday this week, shooting for 11ish, when I'm there to watch and cheer. When they left, he almost immediately fell asleep. I almost can't believe I saw what I saw.

As soon as he woke up, he mouthed, "I want out of this bed." I told him he was absolutely on the way. I'm praying that his frustration and anger will dissipate now that he will be seeing physical progress towards that end.

Christy sent another eMail which he loved, of course. I brought the pile of cards and notes in from home and hung them on his walls; there was no space for them in the SICU. Now when he's up and walking he can read them again. I also hung up the photo of the two of us with him in his white dinner jacket so he and everyone else can see how he looked when he was healthy.

Every day will be an adventure now. I'm ready and so is Jeff.

xxoo M'ree
Organ Donors Save Lives

∞

5/9/2007 No Flowers; No Plants; No Fruit

Oh, boy, this was a tough day from an emotional perspective.

First of all, someone sent flowers. What should have been a very nice thing turned ugly. Unbeknownst to me, Transplant Floor patient rooms may not have flowers, plants or fruit because they can carry fruit flies which can cause infections. When Jeff's Nurse told him she could put them on the nurse's counter, where he could see them from his bed, he got really angry. So please don't send anything other than cards, thank you.

Next, he was very down in the dumps generally. He doesn't see the progress he has already made and the good things to come. He is extremely frustrated because of the things he can't do and he insists he will not get better. He looked so forlorn when the Social Worker was there that she cried. Everyone is trying their best to boost his spirits but nothing is working right now. He told me that the Psychiatrist was there yesterday; that must have happened after I left for the day. I told him that if he wants medication for his spirits, he can have it. He says an emphatic NO. I'll have to catch up with the Psychiatrist so we can strategize; I'll start with an eMail tonight.

When the Physical Therapists arrived, he performed very well. He sat on the edge of the bed, almost able to hold himself up. He did lots of arm exercises. He was pleasant and cooperative. He is happy to do whatever they want from him. I have to believe that when he starts to see progress, he will gain some perspective and cheer up.

The best news is that Jeff's Nurse told him they would install the talking trach today, but that didn't happen before I left. As soon as he can talk, I'll let people know and they can call him. Let's hope he will answer the phone.

There was a zippered canvas tote bag on his shelf. Inside it was: a loose-leaf binder with all sorts of information for liver transplant recipients (it contained a lot of don't do this, don't do that; e.g., don't work in the garden for the first year because you can be exposed to spores, molds, etc.); a carrying case containing a 7-day pill container; sunscreen lotion [anti-rejection meds increase sun sensitivity]; sunscreen lip balm; anti-bacterial hand cleaner; a box containing a watch with the logo of the Gift of Life foundation; and information about how to send a note to the donor's family. I've started putting that together in my mind. You can imagine that it's not an easy project, but I want to do it as soon as I can. I just have to prepare myself for an evening in tears. Maybe tomorrow. I'm spent for today.

Aside: I did ultimately compose and send the letter. It was the most intense writing I have ever done, and the process totally exhausted me. To protect the privacy of the donor's family, I will not include the text.

xxoo M'ree
Organ Donors Save Lives

∞

5/10/2007   Where to Begin

Today was so action-packed that my head is spinning.

Significant: PT came in with the "Lift Team" (i.e., two huge guys). First they got Jeff sitting on the edge of the bed. Then the Lift Team literally lifted him from the bed into the reclining chair. He sat there for just over an hour. He looked pretty comfortable, but his eyes were big with surprise. Then, while he was in the chair…

Very Significant: Three of the Transplant Team Doctors arrived to remove the trach and replace it with a smaller one that would work with the talking valve. The replacement was a little traumatic for Jeff. It was quick and not complicated, but Jeff was nervous to begin with. Then while they were changing it, Jeff started to gag and threw up. The Doctors calmed him and quickly cleaned him up. Then it was done and Jeff was fine, but exhausted. Then, while he was still in the chair…

Fun: Anarie arrived for a visit. Jeff said he was uncomfortable and wanted to get back into bed. He had been in the chair for a little over an hour, which is wonderful. The Lift Team returned, put him back into bed, then Anarie and I went to the cafeteria while the nurses did their daily wound care, etc., etc. Anarie had him not only smiling, but laughing. She has the magic touch, for sure.

Distracting: Two Social Workers stopped in and chatted. Jeff was glad to see them, but it was clear that he was pretty tired.

Most significant: The Speech/Swallow Therapist installed a

Passy-Muir valve, which will let Jeff both speak and eat. Simplistically, it closes off the trach so it's as though the trach is not there. He had Jeff count and then say the months to see if Jeff would be comfortable with it, which he was. Jeff's voice was weak, but it was definitely his voice. Oh, boy, it was great to hear him again. Then he gave Jeff a little applesauce to eat, which had been colored green for suctioning visibility. The objective was that after Jeff swallowed, the Therapist would suction the trach to make sure that no food got caught. Jeff swallowed it fine, but said his throat hurt so much that he didn't want to eat any more. That being the case, the Therapist only suctioned superficially, but no food was caught. He asked Jeff if he was willing to try to swallow some cranberry juice. Jeff said yes, and took a little swig, then said his throat still hurt. The Therapist ordered some anesthetic spray to ease the pain. He took the valve off until tomorrow, when he will try again, hoping that Jeff's throat won't be as sore. The soreness, by the way, is due to a combination of things: the intubations, the suctioning, the time he hasn't used his vocal cords, etc.

Encouraging: The Physical Therapist came in and said that since Jeff had already had a lot of activity today, she would leave him in the bed. She did foot, leg and arm exercises. She said that Jeff is getting stronger already. She also told Jeff that she is figuring out how to get him down to the gym soon. He liked hearing that.

Somewhat upsetting: One of the Transplant Doctors came in to tell us that they want to install a GEJ (gastro-esophageal junction) tube. This is a feeding tube inserted into the belly. It's done in the OR under general anesthesia. Jeff said NO. The Doctor said they are concerned about Jeff's history of aspiration, and that they need to do it so his GI tract will start to work again. Jeff said NO again. The Doctor said he would come back later to talk again. I guess we shall see what we shall see.

Neutral: The Psychiatrist said he would try to visit while I'm there today or tomorrow, but he didn't get there today.

Absolutely mind boggling: A nurse from BMR came in to announce that Jeff would go there next. He will be in their "Medical Rehabilitation" program. He will have a private room to minimize the chance of infections. I have to get Jeff five sets of pants and shirts for therapy sessions. He must take sneakers or lace-up equivalents. They expect to take him there, depending on his progress at HUP, in maybe a week!!! My jaw dropped. Jeff just shook his head NO. He's still in negative mode. The nurse said that she is basing this guestimate on the info in his chart. He has to be eating, of course, and he has to be able to tolerate at least three hours of PT daily, but it's absolutely coming and much sooner than I ever expected. Oh, my goodness! I think I may have been hallucinating.

xxoo M'ree
Organ Donors Save Lives

5/11/2007   Party

Unofficial party, of course. The distinguished guests included our friends Fred, John, Anthony, Maria and Jimmy. Except that Fred arrived and left early; he must have had someplace better to go (just kidding). And the best part is that everyone was unexpected. Well, I would have expected Fred if I'd gotten my messages before he arrived. Anyway, everyone did a great job lifting Jeff's spirits. He smiled a lot.

I was later than usual arriving today. By the time I arrived, both PT and OT had been and gone. They had him sit on the edge of the bed and do leg and arm exercises. They never found a Lift Team to move him into the chair.

He is not using the Passy-Muir valve yet, even though he could. He has a ton of secretions, which makes it both messy and uncomfortable. No one is pressuring him to do it before he is ready.

On the way up to the room, I met the Social Worker, who told me that the Psychiatrist had been to talk with Jeff and that Jeff has agreed to take medication for his depression. I have mixed feelings. It tears at my heart to see him down, but I keep hoping that seeing even a little progress every day will cheer him without the need for more drugs. I have to trust in the Psychiatrist's experienced judgment that depression can impede healing. They can always stop the meds.

When the party guests had about departed, a Transplant

Team Resident showed up to discuss the feeding tube. They actually want to put in a PEG (percutaneous endoscopic gastrostomy) tube, instead of a GEJ tube. It accomplishes the same thing: he will be fed through the tube. Their reasoning is that while the trach is still in place, he has a greater chance of aspirating anything he eats via his mouth. That is not only traumatic in itself, but it contributes to pneumonia, which is especially tough to cure while someone is on anti-rejection drugs. After the PEG tube is in, they will remove the NG tube that is now suctioning from his stomach. Then, when Jeff is up to the recommended feedings via the PEG tube, they will also stop the TPN IV feeding. The PEG tube must physically stay in place for at least six to eight weeks before they remove it. Before that, if it's no longer needed, they would just tie it off. If it's needed longer, that's fine, too. All things considered, the Team says he needs the PEG tube. Jeff finally relented and said ok. The deed will be done on Monday. The procedure just takes 15 minutes, but they have to anesthetize him, and then wake him up afterwards.

Point of General Information: I also met the Transplant Surgeon in the hall; she wasn't wearing her white coat. I congratulated her when I realized that she is unquestionably expecting a baby soon. She is due in two months, which means that when she did Jeff's transplant, she was five months pregnant. She also has two other kids at home. Oh my goodness.

The plan remains to transfer him to BMR next week, assuming all goes well between now and then. I've already shopped for his PT pants, shirts and socks, per instructions from their nurse. To give Jeff some sense of control, I told him that I would bring the stuff in and if he doesn't like it, that I would take it back. Fingers crossed!

xxoo M'ree
Organ Donors Save Lives

∞

5/11/2007   Goofus

No PT today; it's the weekend. Jeff is willing to use the Passy-Muir valve once in a while, but mostly he prefers to leave it off. He seems to feel uneasy about covering the trach and not having the oxygen. That's perfectly ok.

My nephew, Ron, and his wife, Kathy, visited today. Jeff was clearly pleased to see them and gave them a couple of big smiles. Just before they arrived, his Nurses were turning him and cleaning him up when he had a stabbing pain in his leg. The Nurses thought he may have pulled a muscle or some such thing. They gave him a pain med, which immediately made him totally relaxed and comfortable during the visit. After Ron and Kathy left, he became very confused. I'm attributing it to a pain med; his Nurse agreed. Here are some examples: he wanted me to ask his Nurse if the bills had been signed; he wanted to know where the blue box and the red bag were so I could pack in them; he wanted to know how he would get to the car when he's leaving HUP; he wanted me to tell him where the meat was; he wanted me to bring him spoons from the cafeteria. Ok, fine.

This morning I packed Jeff's bag so he's ready to leave for BMR; there won't be time during the week to do it last minute. I washed all the new PT clothes, and had to put his name into everything, like at camp, so they don't lose it. We have to do our own laundry, either there or at home.

The day was very low-keyed. No PT. Jeff was not confused at all. He said his throat is very sore (this would be from the thrush that has until now resisted their attempts to eliminate with an antibiotic). They are giving him an anesthetic throat spray, but it's not helping much. He talks a little with the Passy-Muir valve; they will be leaving it on more every day until he uses it 24/7. He also said that the pain from yesterday hasn't left. He thinks it may be that his hernia has returned. His Nurse is alerting the Transplant Team so they can check it out tomorrow. Thank goodness that he can talk, even a little bit.

Tomorrow they will insert the PEG tube, but as of this minute, we don't know the time.

Christy and TJ will both be here next weekend. TJ from Friday to Sunday; Christy from Saturday to Monday. He will be thrilled to see them, as always. I really hope he's moved by then so they can see the new digs. They will have missed the Transplant Floor entirely, but not that much has transpired there, so that's ok with me.

My niece, Susan, came to my rescue again today by feeding the cats and fish so I could join Anthony and Maria for their family Mother's Day pig out. I'm so blessed to have such support all around.

xxoo M'ree
Organ Donors Save Lives

∞

5/14/2007   Let's Make a Deal

Last night immediately after I shut down the computer, the phone rang. Jeff's Nurse said that they would take him for the PEG tube insertion at 6:10am. They would let me in to see him beforehand if I want. Yes, I did want. So I woke up at 4am today and rushed into town. As soon as I got to Jeff's room, his Nurse told me that the OR wouldn't be available because there had been an emergency. They took him at 9am, and he was back in the room at 1pm. Of course.

The PEG tube went in without a hitch. The NG tube is now out. He has no pain. He's talking better, even without the Passy-Muir valve. He slept the rest of the time I was there, but PT did say they would come around later and try to get him to stand up. Lots of luck to them. The Therapist said that he had been very stubborn the last time they were with him. They wanted him to stand up vs sit up. He insisted he was too weak to stand and anyway he had already been standing up earlier in the day, which was not true. In the end, he got his way and sat.

The nurse from BMR was there and told me they are targeting his move for Wednesday or Thursday, assuming they are sure he can take three hours of PT every day. That remains to be seen.

One minute after she left, a Medicine Doctor arrived to tell me that one of Jeff's blood enzymes is a little elevated and they may have to do a biopsy to check for possible rejection. My antenna went up and my brain started working overtime. Which enzyme? Alkaline phosphatase. Oh, no, that's the one that started this whole liver disease process those many years ago. The very one. Is this the beginning of another cycle? I didn't even ask him that question because I know they don't know. Of course, it's possible. Why even ask? So, anyway, he said that the doctors will discuss it and decide what to do next. If there is rejection going on, it's both treatable and also very slight at this point. Will this jeopardize his impending move to BMR? Depending on what they do to treat it, if it needs treating, it could. Jeff slept through all this, thank goodness. I can't imagine what he would do if he had heard.

So, let's make a deal, Team of Angels. I will trust the doctors and take one step at a time if you will help to keep me calm. OK?

xxoo M'ree
Organ Donors Save Lives

5/15/2007 First They Say They Will and Then They Won't

Remember that old song: "You're Undecided Now, So What Are You Gonna Do"? That was today.

When I was at the coffee cart waiting for my tea to take to Jeff's room, one of the Transplant Team Surgeons walked up to me and said how thrilled she is with Jeff's progress. I told her about the alkaline phosphatase level and the possible biopsy. She told me not to worry about to that. The alk phos post-transplant is totally different from pre-transplant and it's probably not significant. He's making huge strides. I thanked her for making my day and breathed a huge sigh of relief.

When I got to Jeff's room, the first thing he said was that he wanted to do his exercises. So we did both leg and arm. He's very strong.

Jeff's Nurse ran in to tell me that he's set to move tomorrow, Wednesday, at 10am. She said that the Transplant Coordinator would come to the room to see me at 1pm with discharge instructions, meds, etc. I was already set to attend the weekly Liver Transplant Support Group meeting at noon. It's usually only open to the recipients, but the Social Worker wanted me there to talk with them.

The Support Group meeting was a great experience. There were five people who got their transplants from two months to 14 years ago, plus one person who is waiting for a liver-and-lung transplant: a very rare combination. What stories! I'm glad I went and hope Jeff will go sometime.

The Transplant Coordinator arrived carrying a large carton (about the size of two bread boxes) into Jeff's room and went over everything with both of us. Besides the many meds, each of which she explained thoroughly, and the rest of the usual hospital discharge-type directions, there were goodies including: a scale; a digital thermometer; a blood-pressure cuff; a 4x7 day pill holder; a pill splitter; and a tote bag. I felt like I was leaving a trade show with all the stuff you gather while walking through the exhibits. The directions included four Don't-Ever-Do-Again things that I made her read aloud to Jeff so he wouldn't say I made them up: no grapefruit because it has an enzyme that counteracts anti-rejection drugs (he mail-orders Ruby Reds from the Rio Grande valley); no raw fish or shellfish (sushi is his favorite food - now he'll have to eat cooked only, and he could eat his weight in oysters on the half shell); no meat less than well done (if it doesn't move, he'll eat it); and low salt (he salts ham sandwiches). Oh, this will be so hard for him. The Team of Angels will have to give him strength.

Jeff's Nurse told me not to come to HUP tomorrow, but just to meet Jeff at BMR at about 11am. There is nothing that needs to be signed before Jeff leaves. They told me to take everything of Jeff's home, except for his eyeglasses. I took down all the hanging photos and greeting cards. I gave the flowers to a woman who had none and was permitted to have them in her room. I packed everything up and called Christy and TJ with the good news.

After hugging everyone and reassuring Jeff that I would have everything he needs with me tomorrow morning, I left. Before I drove home, I stopped at the florist across the street to send fruit to the nurses' station. Oh, boy, it felt so good to pay for that parking space for the last time.

On the way home, my cell phone said I had a voice mail. The phone number was from HUP. It was Jeff's Nurse, telling me that the move to BMR has been postponed until maybe Thursday or Friday. The Transplant Team Head wants to do a precautionary biopsy before Jeff leaves HUP. He will also check Jeff's gall bladder, and may do a VRCP (volume-rendered cholangiopancreatography) to get a good look, and maybe even put in a stent, if needed, to keep the vein open. Sounded fine to Jeff and me, too. So be it. The biopsy, etc., will happen sometime tomorrow in Interventional Radiology. I'm planning to be there at my usual time; they will call me if I should change it. Oh, and tomorrow they will also start feeding him through the PEG tube.

I'm ready for whatever tomorrow brings. I'm just too tired to get upset.

xxoo M'ree
Organ Donors Save Lives

∞

5/16/2007   Dreaming

We all must be dreaming. This can't be real. I should stress first that Jeff is doing very well overall and looks great. He's awake and alert and is talking when he uses his Passy-Muir valve, sometimes even without it. He's strong and very interested in doing his exercises. He's not showing signs of depression. He's feisty. He's getting better.

This is a simple thing, so I'll start with it. Jeff has c.diff bacteria in his intestines, so he has the poops again and is on antibiotics for that. This is something very common in a hospital, and it's also very communicable. Now, in addition to gowns and gloves, everyone who goes in and out of his room must wash their hands with soap. All the surfaces in his room must be cleaned with bleach.

Nutrition remains a bugaboo. Jeff failed his swallow study a couple of days ago. This means that they are not comfortable putting anything substantive in his stomach, because he might cough it up and aspirate it. They want to avoid that at all costs. So they are using his PEG tube for suction only, and sometimes to give him very small amounts of meds. They will continue TPN IV feedings for the time being. That's fine, taken by itself, but it's jeopardizing his admission to BMR. BMR does not like to take people who are not being fed via their stomachs. No one has said exactly why, but it seems obvious to me that if someone is not eating normally, they will not be able to function as well and maybe won't progress as fast. The Social

Worker is talking to them, but it could be that BMR might refuse to take him at all. One option would be to stay at HUP and use their internal rehab. We just have to see how this plays out.

Today at 7am, they did the liver biopsy. No results yet. During the same outing, they did a scan of his legs to check for potentially life-threatening blood clots, which often form when someone is bedridden for a long time. Oh, no: he has one in each leg. The right one is in the thigh and is only partially occluding the vessel. The left one is behind his knee and is totally occluding the vessel. They must address this immediately, so the clots don't migrate. He will be on heparin (a blood thinner) until they are resolved.

PT came in during the afternoon. They had intended to stand him up, but he was too sleepy from the morning anesthesia. They couldn't do leg exercises because of the clots. They did do arm exercises; he is doing splendidly with those and is making fast progress.

At 4pm today, they took him back downstairs for the VRCP. We'll have the results tomorrow.

With all of this, he won't be discharged from the Transplant Floor until at least Sunday. More likely not until Monday. I'll believe it when I see it.

xxoo M'ree
Organ Donors Save Lives

∞

5/17/2007   Good Question

Jeff continues to improve overall, but not always every single day. Today he said he was nauseous and didn't look too peppy, but he wasn't down in the dumps. He's talking more and more, but doesn't wear his Passy-Muir valve much. He didn't have any PT today because of his nausea combined with the fact that that they don't want him standing until he has been "heparinized" for at least 24 hours since discovering his clots. They brought him new dainty blue foot wraps that are connected to some sort of pump. They have replaced the white pressurized leg wraps, and are supposed to keep the blood flowing in his legs.

The VRCP didn't get done until late in the evening. The original Gastroenterologist did it, which pleased Jeff a lot. The test showed that one of his liver veins was somewhat blocked, so they inserted a stent to open it up. They told me that the blockage could have been the cause of his elevated alk phos (an enzyme that indicates liver function). Now they expect the level to gradually drop down.

There are no results from the biopsy yet.

Jeff is in that limbo land between being really sick and really well. There are a few scenarios for where he goes next and when.

Almost everything depends on something else. The key to everything is his feedings. There has been a ton of discussion about the pros and cons of various approaches. Now they are going to do two tests: one is a dye test of the PEG tube to see if things move down or up. If they move down, that's good. If they move up, they can't start PEG feedings yet. The other test is a gastric volume test; I don't understand the implication of this one, but it must have to do with whether he can eat enough to sustain himself. Regardless, if they feel confident that he can tolerate PEG feedings, they will start right away. This will make his next step easier to arrange. BMR does not want to take him unless he is having at least some PEG feedings. For whatever reason, the Transplant Team would rather not have him stay at HUP for rehab. There is yet another option, which would be a sort-of half-way house. This would be a facility that provides complete nursing care, but also gives more PT than the Transplant Floor. There are two: one in Philadelphia and one in West Chester. From one of those, he would then go to BMR. I'm not thrilled with this option, and neither is the Social Worker, because the HUP teams would not have as close oversight as they do now, even though they would be involved.

Everyone, including the insurance company, wants him to leave HUP when he doesn't need that level of care, but no one wants him to go anywhere before he's really ready. As usual, Jeff's whole disease process has been extremely unusual. This makes everyone act very cautiously, which I appreciate. They know that my bottom line question is the same question that Jeff always asks: "If *your* butt was in this bed, what would you do?"

xxoo M'ree
Organ Donors Save Lives

∞

5/18/2007   Is That You, God?

TJ arrived at around lunchtime to stay until Sunday morning.
His face absolutely lit up when he saw how good Jeff looks. And it
was so great to see Jeff smile. He loves his children so much.
Christy arrives tomorrow to stay until Monday afternoon.

Jeff had a couple of bouts of nausea today; who knows why?
Probably it was induced by one or a combination of drugs. His
extreme pooping continues. Other than that, he's doing better every
day and clearly getting stronger. He asked me where his manicurist
was. I told him that tomorrow, when it should be quieter, I would do
both his hands and his feet.

The Psychiatrist came by to visit (twice, actually) but
never got to talk to Jeff because of the nausea episodes. He and I
talked briefly, and I told him that Jeff was doing better emotionally.
He said that it's surely not because of the drugs, because they
wouldn't be effective yet. He said that he still wants Jeff on the drugs
on general principles. I'm ok with that because I wouldn't want to
see anything put him into the pit.

The Social Worker visited for a while and we had some good

distracting conversation. It's hard to imagine how anyone could do a better job than she does. What a gift she has, and what a big heart.

The Transplant Team Head and another Team Doctor rounded. The Transplant Team Head told us that the biopsy results showed a very slight rejection, but quickly said that in a healthy population if you did 10 biopsies, one person would show the same result. They will not do anything about it, but will, of course, watch it. The stent will resolve the slight blockage in the liver vein. The clots in Jeff's legs are being taken care of with the heparin. The Head said that they so want to move Jeff to BMR, probably on Monday. He continued that he heard about the other options for next steps, but that BMR is definitely the best place for Jeff. I told him I understood that BMR doesn't want to take Jeff while he's only on TPN feedings. He very calmly said that the TPN feedings should only be for about two more weeks, and that he would negotiate with BMR, and that he always gets what he wants. OK, fine.

Later in the afternoon, the Physical Therapists arrived and had him start with arm and leg exercises. They also had him comb his hair and wash his face. He was definitely pleased to do that. Then, with the help of two Physical Therapists and two nurses, Jeff sat up on the edge of the bed. When he didn't realize it, they let go of him. He stayed sitting for a good while without their help. At one point, he even lifted his hand off the bed to point at something and kept his balance. It's as if his body finally remembered how to do it. I was sitting in the corner where he couldn't see me watching with tears running down my cheeks. Since I was behind him, I got a good look at his back. He's put back a lot of weight, so the TPN is doing its job. Next they wanted him to stand. He resisted. They insisted. He stood three times, with lots of help. He never did get completely vertical, but at least he knows what it feels like. His calves are now thinner than mine, which is saying something because his measured 16" last summer when he bought riding boots. I wonder if they will ever get back to their pre-transplant hugeness. The Physical Therapists said that since it's possible that Jeff may move on Monday, they will try their best to do more PT on Saturday and Sunday.

I can hardly wait.

xxoo M'ree
Organ Donors Save Lives

∞

5/19/2007   A Few Words

Christy arrived on schedule, so the three of us were with Jeff all day. It was very quiet. PT never arrived. No doctors rounded. Jeff said he was nauseous but did not vomit. To talk, he preferred to hold his finger over the trach opening vs wearing the Passy-Muir. He seemed not to be feeling too great overall. His color was pretty ashen, and I alerted his Nurse before we left.

We're taking TJ to the airport before we go to HUP because his flight is early. Christy and I will hold the fort today. I'm hoping that PT visits, because as of this minute, Jeff is still set to transfer to

BMR on Monday.

Stay tuned.

xxoo M'ree
Organ Donors Save Lives

∞

5/20/2007   Looking Good for a Move Tomorrow

Christy and I dropped TJ off at the airport on the way to HUP. Jeff was much more chipper today overall. He was even joking with his Nurses. He still said he's nauseous, but didn't actually get sick. It was still quiet. PT still never arrived. They have been giving Jeff water via his PEG tube, and it's been working perfectly.

The Transplant Team Head and two of his underlings rounded. The Transplant Team Head told us that he did get his way. BMR agreed to take Jeff as he is, and they are set to move him tomorrow, provided that there is a private room available (they only have three). Also, they can do another speech/swallow study as early as tomorrow at HUP or right away at BMR. As soon as Jeff passes that study, he can have water and even food by mouth. Jeff really wants a drink of water. He wants it now.

We are to call the nurse's station at 9:30am tomorrow to find out whether he will move and if so, what time. Then Christy and I will know where to go and when. We have his duffel bag in the car's wayback. Even if it doesn't happen tomorrow, we know it's only a matter of days. Looking back, Jeff is light years beyond where he was even a couple of weeks ago. His transplant was a gift that keeps on giving, as they say. I'm so grateful.

xxoo M'ree
Organ Donors Save Lives

∞

5/21/2007   Would You Believe: Not Yet?

It's true. He's not moving to BMR yet. When we called in the morning, Jeff's Nurse said that his heparin level was not yet "therapeutic" and he cannot move until that level is achieved. They are guesstimating that it will be 36-48 hours. Arrrrrrgh! This is so frustrating.

Christy and I spent the day with Jeff. Her flight was delayed, so she was able to stay on after I left for the day. Good for both her and Jeff.

In the morning, we ran into the BMR/HUP Liaison Nurse in the hall and she confirmed that Jeff does have to be at least weaning off of the TPN before they will take him. He is only getting the TPN at night now, and they have continued water boluses into his PEG tube, but he hasn't gotten any food via the PEG tube yet. The Transplant Team Head said that they would start PEG feeds tonight. Let's pray hard that he tolerates them ok. He will be emotionally crushed if he can't move soon.

After I left, the Speech/Swallow Therapist came to do a second study. Luckily, Christy was still there so she reported to me via phone afterwards. He failed: he didn't completely swallow the green-colored applesauce and said that it made him nauseous. He asked the Therapist what he could do to pass the next time. The Therapist told him that he should use the Passy-Muir valve as much as possible and get comfortable coughing up his lung secretions vs being suctioned. Christy said that after the Therapist left, Jeff asked to keep the valve on. He is really motivated to pass the test. He's been asking for water to drink, but the Transplant Team Head said "no compromise". Too much danger of aspiration and a huge setback, plus possible pneumonia. He accepted that.

As the Transplant Team predicted so long ago in the SICU, there were two challenges: breathing, which is virtually resolved, and nutrition, which remains an issue. His digestive system has to be completely primed and restarted. Sort of like a car that ran out of gas.

Christy said that Jeff was ok when she left. I'm glad for that, because I hate to see him sad. I'm very glad that Christy and TJ got to visit us again. And I'm thankful to their better halves and kids who missed them for the weekend.

I need to be in my local office tomorrow, so my report will be via phone information. The nurses know that if I need to get there, they can call my cell. Don't even think it.

xxoo M'ree
Organ Donors Save Lives

∞

5/22/2007   Remote Newscast

Today I worked in the local office, so I didn't get to HUP. I spoke with Jeff's Nurse in the morning, at midday and just now.

They started his PEG feedings (small: 10ml/hr) at 3am, and he has tolerated them without any problems. There have been no "residuals" (what is left in his stomach after a time), so it means his digestive system is processing the food as it should. This is the first hurdle in getting to BMR. He said he feels a little bloated, but that's to be expected given that it's been a long time since he's had anything in his stomach. Overnight, he will also get TPN via IV.

PT came today and he did leg and arm exercises and also sat up on the edge of the bed. His Nurse was present and said that she never expected that he would do so well. The Therapists said he's progressing fast.

His heparin level had changed very little between yesterday and today, so it's still not therapeutic. Jeff's Nurse was careful to tell me that different people react very differently to heparin, and it's possible that just one more dose could put him into the therapeutic range. Once that happens, he's set to transfer to BMR, provided they have a bed. His Nurse says maybe by Thursday. So we wait patiently for the magic moment.

xxoo M'ree
Organ Donors Save Lives

∞

5/23/2007   The Impatient Disease

As of today, they are targeting Tuesday, May 29th, for moving to BMR. Jeff's heparin level has barely changed, so that's the holdup. He probably doesn't need that much time, but the holiday weekend is coming up and they won't move him then. His PEG feedings are going great. We're looking at it this way: this just gives him more time to gather strength before the trials of steady PT.

He asked me to bring his beard trimmer tomorrow so he looks more groomed. It shall be done.

He also asked me which car I had driven to HUP. I said that we only have one car: the Volvo. He wanted to know where his Chevy is. I said that the only cars we've had together have been a Toyota, a Subaru and the Volvo, plus his Ford truck at one point. I asked him if he had had a Chevy when he was married to the kids' mother (over 25 years ago), and he said yes: three. Then he twirled his finger next to his temple a la cuckoo. It's as if time has gotten compressed in his mind in some respects. That's so interesting. The Psychiatrist said that this would possibly happen, and that it should just disappear in time.

He talked a lot today, and it's possible to understand him almost all the time, even without the Passy-Muir valve on. His throat is getting stronger. He was very disappointed that he failed the second speech/swallow test. I reminded him that he was intubated for a long time and hadn't used his throat for even longer and reassured him that it would work again soon. It will, too.

PT didn't come today, which was disappointing. Maybe tomorrow. It's too bad that both of us have the impatient disease. Patience is another lesson we can both learn from this whole ordeal.

xxoo M'ree
Organ Donors Save Lives

5/24/2007   Somewhat Scared

When I walked into Jeff's room, there he sat, upright in the cushy chair, as though he had always been there. The Physical Therapists were just standing nearby, watching and praising him. They had helped him into the chair, of course, but he was managing just fine. Before this, he had done his arm and leg exercises in the bed, had washed his face and combed his hair, and sat on the edge of the bed for five minutes. While he was sitting in the chair, I took advantage of his position to trim his beard as he requested yesterday. He stayed in the chair for half an hour, when he said his butt hurt (one sore is still open, but is healing). Before they could get him back in bed, he got sick to his stomach and lost whatever was in there. It's always something.

The Physical Therapists have booked him into the gym for tomorrow afternoon, while I'm there to watch. The plan is to take him down there and put him into a chair-like contraption that will stand him up while he's strapped in. This is to 1) make sure he doesn't fall, and 2) make him feel safe while he's standing. He's very much afraid to try it because he says he's too weak. He is weak, but not too weak for that. They kept explaining to him that it's natural to be afraid of this after so long in bed and that they won't let any harm come to him. We could tell from his face that he's not buying it yet.

Later I learned that he had a pretty severe coughing spell at 5:30am. They were concerned that he had aspirated again and did an x-ray, which looked better than one week ago, so it was a false alarm. Because of this, though, they will be extra careful with his PEG feeds, and will go even slower than they were already going. We're all hoping this doesn't jeopardize his projected moving date.

His heparin level is very slowly inching up to therapeutic level, where is must be before he goes to BMR. His Nurse explained to me that they started with heparin, and then they added another drug, which should make the level increase faster. Later they will stop one of the two drugs. His Nurse said that she doesn't understand how it works, so neither do I.

After he took a long nap, he said he thinks he isn't ready to go to BMR yet. He's so worried that he won't be able to handle the

PT. He needs confidence. Everyone is sending him strength vibes tomorrow.

xxoo M'ree
Organ Donors Save Lives

∞

5/25/2007   The Magnificent EasyStand

First the vitals. He's now on almost no oxygen support. The Transplant Team rounded. They talked about removing the trach completely within the next couple of days. This won't have an effect on his aspiration risk, which revolves around him coughing up what may be in his stomach and then breathing it into his lungs. They are still very intent on preventing that.

Because of the big coughing yesterday morning, they took a break from the PEG feeds until this afternoon, when they restarted them at 150ml every four hours. When he has been at 300 ml for 24 hours without problems, he's ok to move to BMR, and not before. It seems that the Transplant Team Head didn't really get what he wanted this time, and I'll not mention it to him. Jeff may get to that level by Tuesday, but it's not a sure thing.

His heparin level actually went down 0.1 point. Heparin, apparently, is a weird drug and this happens. They are not concerned. Whatever it is, it won't keep him from going to BMR. Also, one of the Transplant Team Doctors simplistically explained heparin vs Coumadin. To begin with, heparin is only available for either injection or IV; Coumadin is only available in pill form. Heparin is effective very quickly and Coumadin takes a while. So when someone needs more than an incidental administration, they start with heparin and then switch to Coumadin. Allrighty, then.

Here's today's biggie: it was gym day. Two strong male Physical Therapists loaded him onto a gurney and down we all went. He was definitely nervous, but he wanted to go. The female Physical Therapist met us there. The first thing they did - before he was able to see it and freak out - was to install him into the EasyStand. I could never do it justice with a description, so here's a picture of a similar model, cut from the web:

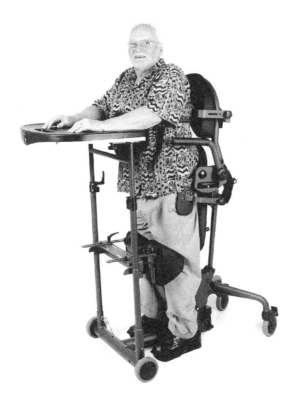

The model at HUP also has a head and back rest attachment, plus special holding pads that go against the hips on each side, as well as yet another set of pads that go on each side of the ribs. They strap the person in with big Velcro bands around the hips and chest. You get the idea: there is no way the person is going anywhere. Then they use the gear-shift-type lever and ratchet the person into a standing position, with their chest against the part the model is holding onto. There is a flat table just above that. When they got Jeff up, they put a full-length mirror in front of him so he could both see himself and adjust himself from side to side. He tends to lean towards the right. They also let him comb his hair. He stood for 11 minutes before he said his legs were cramping. Just think of it: he hasn't stood up for almost three months. He did fine and I think he was actually surprised by how well he did. After that, they put him back onto the gurney and did leg and arm exercises. They also gave him a container of putty to use for hand exercises back in his room.

He was totally tuckered out by the time we got back to the room, so I left just after they got him re-situated in the bed. I'll see what he has to say tomorrow about the gym experience. I hope it's given him more confidence that he really will recover. Sometimes I think he doubts it, and I'm not surprised.

xxoo M'ree
Organ Donors Save Lives

5/26/2007   A Saturday With News

PEG feeds are going fine. They plan to have him up to 300 ml/4 hrs by Monday. I'm hoping for a move on Tuesday, but I promise not to be crushed if it doesn't happen. I've finally learned that lesson.

The heparin is doing what it should. He's up to 1.8 today; the target is 2. Looking good.

They are still working towards removing the trach. Decanulating, it's called, medically. He's on humidified room air vs oxygen now.

He was very comfortable today and he slept a lot. His Nurses sat him up on the edge of the bed. He did fine, but needed to be laid back down before long. He said he is still tired from the gym.

I called Christy on my cell from his room and he actually talked with her a little using the speakerphone while I held it. This is the first time he's spoken on the phone since February. He liked it, but his voice is weak.

He is definitely both anxious *to go* and *about going* to BMR. When anyone mentions it, he gets quiet and looks very serious. He's afraid he can't cut it with the rehab. He has to cross this bridge by himself. I'll walk behind him with the Team of Angels.

xxoo M'ree
Organ Donors Save Lives

∞

5/27/2007   Inching Up

PEG feeds are still going perfectly. The goal was 300 ml/4 hrs. Today he's getting 200 ml/4 hrs. They will increase it tomorrow, too; I'm not sure to what level.

His heparin level (read "INR") is 1.9; target is 2.

He sat on the edge of the bed again today. He swung his own legs over. They had to raise his body, but he held himself up with almost no support. He's getting stronger every day, even with the relatively minimal exercise he is getting.

He is so afraid of going to BMR. He told me he wouldn't be able to do the PT and that they will have to send him back. His Nurses are all encouraging him. I am, too, but you know that what I say doesn't do any good because I don't have credibility with him for this stuff. I can only pray like crazy that his fear lessens so it's not so hard on him. He's been through enough without this anxiety.

Tomorrow will be quiet again because it's also a HUP holiday.

xxoo M'ree
Organ Donors Save Lives

∞

5/28/2007   Will He? Won't He?

PEG feeds are still perfect. He's up to 250 ml/4 hrs without a hitch. I understand that BMR wants 300 ml before the move, so I'm assuming it won't happen tomorrow, but no one knows for certain either way. I'll have to wait until after morning rounds (at roughly 9am) to find out. We've agreed that I'm to call them at 9:30 if they have not called me earlier. I'm set to handle either agenda and the car is willing to drive in either direction. His bag is still packed from the false alarm.

The INR level went down to 1.8, so he's still below the target of 2. No one is concerned.

Today they sat him in the Transplant Floor's equivalent of the SICU's Pink Chair. It's larger, to accommodate the heavy bariatric patients who are on the other side of the floor, and it's black. And it folds flat like a gurney. They sidled it up to the bed, used the famous rolling board to shift him, and then sat him up for 40 minutes. He was fine the whole time.

Also today we called both Christy and TJ using my cell phone in speaker mode, and he talked to both of them. They were both thrilled and so was he.

Other possibilities for tomorrow if he stays at HUP are another speech/swallow test plus the decanulation.

This feels like a classic TV end-of-season cliffhanger. Tune in tomorrow for the next exciting episode.

xxoo M'ree
Organ Donors Save Lives

∞

5/29/2007   He Didn't

Ok, the rule (directly to my ears from the mouth of the
BMR/HUP Liaison Nurse) is that his PEG feeds have to be at 300
ml/4 hrs for 24 hours before he moves. He got his first 300 ml dose
at 11:30 this morning. The BMR/HUP Liaison Nurse said that she
requested a private room for tomorrow; the earliest he will go is
tomorrow afternoon. She also said that since he's off the IV heparin,
that's ok with them. I don't know what his INR was today, but it
doesn't matter. So this is another cliffhanger day.

Having said that, I was pretty disconcerted this morning
because when I arrived, Jeff was totally confused. First he told me to
check "the other room" to see if we'd gotten his things out. He
insisted that he had left HUP and was at our house, on the dining
room table, when an ambulance brought him to this new room. He
wanted me to tell him how they had gotten him from the table into
the ambulance. He also told me to check behind the other bed,
because he had put my walking stick on the floor there and then
forgot it. I'm sure he had been dreaming, or, at least, I hope he had
been dreaming. His Nurse said that he was confused for them earlier

in the morning, too. They had two doctors talk to him, but the doctors said that he had a perfectly normal conversation with them. How would they know what was normal? She said she told them that the conversation might have been fine, but the content didn't make sense. They didn't think anything needed to be done; they said he was probably just waking up. At any rate, he was fine after that episode. I guess I'm just not supposed to relax totally.

Now, having said that, too, three great things happened today:

- First, they stopped his IV TPN. His only nutrition is now via the PEG tube. No more IVs left. Hallelujah!

- Then, PT sat him in the bariatric chair and he stayed there very comfortably for 75 minutes, until he said his butt hurt. His one remaining pressure ulcer is now smaller than a dime, but they are still treating it very conscientiously. Anyway, he was chatting and joking with the PT people; it was the first time he's acted close to his usual self and I was very encouraged. Later, when I asked him how he felt sitting up for that long, he said he would rather have been up walking around. I was really thrilled to hear him say that.

Next, while he was in the bariatric chair, two Transplant Team Doctors removed the trach. I don't know what I expected, but it was a total non-event. They just opened the Velcro holding the strap around his neck and pulled the cannula out of his throat. It literally took five seconds and Jeff didn't feel anything at all. Then they put gauze over the hole and taped it. They said that the hole will close itself totally within a couple of weeks (somewhat longer than it would take if he wasn't on anti-rejection drugs). He can't drink or eat anything until he passes a speech/swallow test, which will be done at BMR. The only negative is that he can't talk well now, because some air still gets through the gauze and the remaining hole. If he holds his hand over the gauze it's better, but it's not as good as it was with the Passy-Muir. It will improve as the days pass and the hole closes. No more: strap around his neck; trach sticking out of his neck; Passy-Muir valve; trach collar and oxygen tube connecting him to the wall; incessant hissing from the oxygen; and wet pads around his trach from the excess humidification. Except for the PEG tube, which is only connected to the food dispensing machine when it's in use, he's free at last!

I'm satisfied to have his packed bag just living in the car now. When he goes, he goes.

xxoo M'ree
Organ Donors Save Lives

∞

5/30/2007   Today He Did

He's really moved, folks! He's in his new home.

Visiting hours are Mon - Fri: 4pm - 9pm; Sat: noon - 9pm; Sun: 10am - 9pm. He can have visitors during any of those times.

In theory he can have flowers, but there is literally no place to put them in his huge room because the windowsill is only about 4" wide and the only shelf is not much wider. He's just going to be sleeping and showering in there anyway. I've already hung all of the cards, notes and family photos on the walls. His labeled clothing is in the closets; his toiletries are in the bathroom. He's in the bed.

This is how the day went. I arrived at HUP at 11am, and his Nurse told me that the ambulance was to pick him up at 1pm. Since he tends to get carsick, they gave him an anti-nausea drug well in advance of the trip. I rushed around calling people, ordering a final fruit basket for the PT/OT people who worked so hard to prepare him for moving, and I visited the SICU to tell the staff. The Social Worker was in his room when I returned, and she stayed with us until the ambulance really did arrive at about 2pm. Traffic and parking delay. After big hugs and goodbyes, we drove to BMR.

BMR really does look like a country club without sand traps. Acres and acres of rolling fields and trees with subtle low-rise buildings, including a big greenhouse for horticulture therapy. His private room has a western exposure, looking out onto beautiful landscaping with a big free-form pond and fountain, complete with terraces and walking trails. Lots of people outside doing things. Generally peaceful and uplifting.

It took until about 5:30pm to get him situated. His Nurse weighed him, using a huge rolling metal framework. They put a stretcher-like thing onto the bed, rolled him onto it, hooked it to the framework and ratcheted it up until he was suspended above the bed. He weighs 197.3, including a lot of remaining ascites and some edema in his feet and ankles. His healthy pre-transplant weight was about 205. They measured his calves: right is 32 cm (12.6 inches); left is 29 cm. This was pretty horrifying to me, because before the transplant, they were about 16 inches. They changed the bandage on his throat. His Nurse said the ENT Doctors taught her to do it differently. She made an X over the hole with tape (which helps to force it to close), then covered it with gauze, and then taped over the whole thing. Now he can talk better. They cleaned him up and changed his gown. He was exhausted. I hope he's exhausted enough to sleep tonight rather than fret about tomorrow.

Tonight at 7pm a doctor was to round and write the orders for his nutrition, meds, etc. His Nurse said that patients get showers every other night. They said that since he hasn't really bathed since February, they would give him a shower tonight. The shower is a great big walk-in version with a chair. He said he was too tired. Tomorrow we'll see who won that one. Whenever they do the speech/swallow test and he passes it, he can start to have drink and food by mouth. I'm sure they will start very slowly and probably with appetizing delights like Jell-O. Yum!

The daily drill is: wake at 7am, start PT at 9am, break for lunch, continue PT, stop for dinner and the evening. They continue PT on the weekends, but not as much. When I arrive each day, I have to ask at the front desk to find out where he is at the moment.

They suggest the caregiver to spend as much time there as possible for encouragement, regardless of official visiting hours. My personal drill will be to work from 5am to 1pm, feed the critters and go out there until after rush hour is over.

I'm excited and a little in shock, to be honest. It hasn't sunk in yet. Maybe it will after I get some sleep myself. I'd better stay alert so I don't automatically drive to HUP.

xxoo M'ree
Organ Donors Save Lives

∞

5/31/2007   Evaluation

This was a day of assessments. The PT, OT, Psych, and Speech/Swallow Therapists all evaluated him. I was only present for the speech/swallow test, which he failed. His speech is so gurgly that the Therapist said he is definitely not swallowing strongly enough to start mouth feedings. And we learned that the gradual process will start with pureed food, e.g., applesauce, vs liquids. Liquids have no weight, so they go right down; this increases the aspiration hazard unless the person can swallow fast and strongly. The therapist may recommend a future radiation test where they mix applesauce with barium to track its progress as it's swallowed. This will tell them if there is anything at all amiss. For that, he would have to go down the road to Paoli Hospital.

There was a bit of a bump in that the HUP med list included a stool softener, which was intended to be given if/when needed. Somehow, they just gave it to him regularly, which caused just what you are thinking. Not exactly what he needed.

It was bad enough that the only PT they could do was in the bed. There is now a wheelchair in his room. I asked if I could take him for a walk around the grounds, but since he didn't get out of bed during the day, they weren't permitted to transfer him into the chair. Tomorrow.

Also, he didn't get his shower last night, so it's now set for tomorrow.

Emotionally, he's absolutely petrified. He knows it, and he also knows that he's very anxious. He cries, he complains, he worries aloud about issues that don't even exist. I've never seen him like this and I'm at a loss to know what to say to calm him. I kept telling him that he will be fine and that he has to trust that they will do everything possible to help him. He called me early in the morning to ask when I would arrive. When I told him at about 2 o'clock, he said he didn't like that. I actually do believe that he's better off without me for some of these first efforts. He has to feel confident that he can do it himself. Which he can. I'm convinced that he'll be fine once he has actually started.

Tomorrow will be the first day of concentrated effort. I wish it were already over so he could get on with it.

Hey, Time, can you fly a little faster please?

xxoo M'ree
Organ Donors Save Lives

∞

6/2/2007   Deconditioned

Oh. That's the word for Jeff's status: "deconditioned". I looked it up on the web: "To decline from a condition of physical fitness, as through a prolonged period of inactivity or, in astronauts, through weightlessness in space. To lose physical fitness". That pretty well sums it up.

Today started with him calling me on the phone in a state of high anxiety. He said he hadn't slept all night because he was scared to death, though he couldn't tell me of what exactly. He wanted reassurance, which I tried to give him. I answered all his questions as best I could and promised him that I was there in spirit and would be there after lunch. I hung up and prayed that he gets the strength to somehow make it through this day.

When I arrived at 2pm, he was in bed, almost asleep, dressed in his exercise clothes but shoeless. He seemed pretty relaxed, but clearly tired out physically. The schedule said that a PT person would be in his room from 2-3 for a working session, which would be his last for the day. He'd already had a full morning and early afternoon of OT and PT. The difference between the two, by the way, is that PT is for physical abilities, e.g., sitting, standing, walking, etc., while

OT is for life skills, e.g., bathing, brushing teeth, cooking, etc.

His therapy had included sitting in his special wheelchair for two hours. It's a tilting chair, that can sort-of recline. It had been specially adjusted by "Bill-the-wheelchair-guy" to fit his height. He also did tons of exercises in his room. The therapy session I witnessed was more exercises in the bed and then sitting on the edge of the bed for about half an hour. One bump was that he was nauseous sitting up and lost whatever was in his stomach. I'm guessing it was as much from nerves as from anything else. He sat through it, though, and held himself up very well.

After all that, his Nurse gave him a shower. His first since February. He said he was too exhausted to go. His Nurse said she was the boss and that he had no choice. She was, indeed. She and a helper literally shifted him into a rolling shower chair and wheeled him into the bathroom. I left the room to get a drink while the deed was accomplished. When I came back, he was already back in bed, looking very spiffy, calm and relaxed. And tired. I helped him brush his teeth, with his own toothbrush and toothpaste, for the first time since February. Since he swore that he wouldn't swallow the water, his Nurse let me give him a cup of water to rinse his mouth like a real person. You could tell by his face that he was feeling empowered. Then he promptly fell asleep.

When it was time for me to leave, I woke him up. He said he felt much better and that it was ok for me to go. The worst is over now.

xxoo M'ree
Organ Donors Save Lives

∞

6/2/2007   How Sore is He?

Pretty darned sore, that's how sore. He said he didn't sleep last night, but I'll bet he will tonight. Today he had a lot of PT. Not sure what he did before I arrived, but with me, we went across to the gym where he helped get himself from the wheelchair onto a big mat that hydraulically raises and lowers to fit the need. Then he did a lot of reaching up and out to each side to take a cone I held out, and then putting it down next to him on the opposite side. His right arm is almost normal, but his left arm is very limited in movement up and out. Then, they stood him up - not once, but twice – using a frame not quite as sophisticated as the EasyStand. Both times he stood up, with lots of help from two people, by himself vs being ratcheted. And he stood for a good while each time. I was actually a little shocked that he had that much strength.

After all that, I took him outside for a half-hour roll around the grounds. He really wanted to go. He liked looking at the plants, but I honestly think he was way too tired to be excited to be outside for the first time since his ambulance ride from HUP to BMR. The fact that it was over 90 degrees and humid didn't encourage us to stay long.

By the time they got him back into bed, he was complaining

that his ribs were terribly sore, so they got him some pain meds.
Then he was cold, so they got him out of his exercise clothes and
back into a hospital gown. He was in tears. My take is that
he's simply totally exhausted from the physical and emotional stress.
We covered him with blankets and he went to dreamland. I sure
hope that he's not in so much pain tomorrow that he doesn't want to
do his morning PT. There is none in the afternoon on Sundays.

Looking back to last Saturday, this week has been gigantic.
No wonder he's spent. I'm spent, too.

xxoo M'ree
Organ Donors Save Lives

∞

6/3/2007   Whooped

Today he slept about 99% of the time I was there. He's just
plain whooped. He had therapy all morning; I don't know what,
exactly, but his Nurse said they worked him hard. It was all in his
room, so there would not have been any standing. It's funny, but
when he sleeps, he must be having vivid dreams because he moves a
lot and even talks. I'm sure that's why he was so confused those
couple of mornings when he was still at HUP.

I learned today that he's getting 3600 calories daily with his
PEG tube feeds. No wonder he's gaining weight.

He's also gaining fluid: ascites and edema both. I'm

wondering what the doctor will do about it? I'll ask tomorrow.

I'm looking forward to seeing how he seems tomorrow. If he's lucky, he will be losing his anxiety as he gains strength and confidence.

xxoo M'ree
Organ Donors Save Lives

∞

6/4/2007   Settling In

Yesterday, before I arrived, two sets of our friends visited: Anarie and Fred, and Margaret and Galen. He told me they were there but I wanted to confirm the facts before I reported. Each of them said that he was in fine spirits while they were there. It's my sense that he does his best to put on a happy face for guests. That's fine with me. Maybe he will convince himself.

Today when I arrived his room was empty. I found the schedule on his tray table and saw that he would be having OT in the dining room. I went in and there he was, dressed and sitting in his wheelchair at a card table, using the "hand bicycle". It's what it sounds like: two pedals you hold onto and work like a bicycle. It has adjustable resistance, so you can make it tougher as you get stronger. He did five minutes forward and again backward. He cried when he saw me.

After that, we went into the gym for PT. He transferred

himself, with a little help, to the up/down mat. Now he can sit without support and balance himself just fine. He stood up, again with some help, twice. Then he sat down and kicked a ball the Therapist rolled to him. The idea is to get his weight off of each side to help with balancing skills. By then he was exhausted.

Back to bed to sleep until I left. While he was sleeping, the Psychologist came in. She has been visiting him daily, but I've never been there at that time. We chatted for a while. She said he's depressed (which is normal and expected for someone who has been through what he has), but seems to be improving a little. I agree with that assessment. She will keep close tabs on him, especially because he said he doesn't want meds. Maybe she can get him to articulate what is at the heart of his anxiety. It seems to be lessening, but it shows up from time to time.

His ascites is getting worse instead of better. His edema is improving. I asked his Nurse if it could possibly be rejection, and she said no, and that they are watching it closely. We also discussed how much progress he has made in less than a week. It's a whole lot.

When I woke him to say goodnight, we called Christy and TJ. It's a gift that he can talk with them. He wouldn't be able to answer his own phone yet because he isn't able to maneuver to get to it.

Tomorrow, I should be able to talk with his Case Manager,

the equivalent of the HUP Social Worker. I want to see what they are thinking about his progress, what their projection is for his stay, etc. I know it's as much a mystery as it was at HUP. Personally, I'll feel a lot better when his spirits seem back to normal. I'm prepared for a wait.

xxoo M'ree
Organ Donors Save Lives

∞

6/5/2007   Better Day

No tears today! That's a great step in the right direction.

When I arrived today he was in the gym. He stood up once but couldn't make it the second time. That was after almost a whole morning of PT, so it was ok. They are going to try a different stand tomorrow.

Then we went down to Speech Therapy, where they taught us more than I thought there was to know about swallowing, plus tips for mouth care without putting a lot of liquid in the mouth.

Next stop was OT, where he did lots of arm exercises with a long, fat dowel wrapped with a weight. I'm amazed at his progress. Then, for the first time without help, he put on his hooded zip-front sweatshirt and took it off again. Then he started learning how to take his slippers off and put them on with a long-handled grabber and a long shoehorn. His ascites is preventing him from bending at the waist in the wheelchair, his edema is making his slippers tight, and he has trouble lifting his feet off the ground, so you can imagine he has some skill to gain. Lastly, he practiced kicking a ball with either foot, to help strengthen his legs.

Then it was time for a shower, after which he went promptly to dreamland until I left. While he was asleep, his Case Manager came in and we talked. They had his one-week review this morning. Given how he has done so far, they are guesstimating four to six weeks at BMR. They re-evaluate this every week. Discharge criteria are one of two: either he meets his goals (which have yet to be established), or he stops making progress for about two to three weeks straight. He could potentially be discharged while he is still being fed via the PEG tube, which surprised me a bit. Assuming that they discharge him to home, they send along whatever equipment he needs, e.g., a walker, cane, etc. It's possible he could need some outpatient visits. Time will tell.

It appears to me that he is very motivated to improve, so he works hard. On the other hand, he tends to procrastinate starting the exercises, and sometimes he delays by finding other things to concentrate on, such as a fraying seam on his sweatshirt. If he gets tired and says he can't do any more, the Therapists can usually get him to continue by encouraging him or directly asking him to try again. They are very good at their jobs, and it's easy to see why BMR has the reputation they do.

One of his Nurses in particular is a task master and seems not to have an empathetic bone in her body, but she is very skilled; she has been there for 10 years. I'm trying to warm her up. Yesterday, she told me that she thinks she may be hardened to the patients' feelings, but she has learned that if she pushes the patients, they improve faster than if she doesn't. I don't know about that yet. Anyway, his other Nurses are all both warm and capable.

Next Tuesday, Jeff will go back to HUP via ambulance for a follow-up visit. I'll drive there from home and meet up with him. I'm chomping at the bit for that appointment.

xxoo M'ree
Organ Donors Save Lives

∞

6/6/2007   Crabby and Confused

Physically, Jeff seemed stronger today to both me and the Physical Therapist. He was more engaged when there was conversation, by which I mean that he looked at the person he was speaking to, rather than looking somewhere else. He also seemed to have more energy.

He had PT all morning, and even put on his own shirt while getting dressed. He did lots of leg and arm exercises. He refused to stand, though, saying that he was both weak and sore from yesterday. That could be true, but it was disappointing nonetheless. The Therapist told him that tomorrow they would take him to the first floor gym (that's the very big one) where they have a leg bicycle that can be used while sitting in a wheelchair. The idea is to build up his leg muscles. Remember that he's a tall, heavy man, despite having lost so much weight. It takes a lot of strength for him to stand.

I was there for the OT, part of which was co-facilitated by the Psychologist. As the session went on, he became more and more difficult for the Therapist. By that, I mean that she would tell him to do something, and he would want to do something totally different. Also, he would stubbornly insist on doing something a different way from what the Therapist wanted. She said to me that she was seeing some "behavior issues" in him which she was purposely ignoring as "tough love". She very calmly and firmly made him look at her and explained exactly what she wanted and why, including pointing out how if he did it the way she wanted, it would be a lot easier. Then she just made him do it. And he was able to do everything she asked, maybe not perfectly, but almost.

Then we went back to his room, where his Nurse greeted me telling me that he had been both confused and in a bad mood in the morning. She said that the bad mood was likely due to his not feeling like he can control much of anything. After he was in bed, he asked me how many of the fountain pens in the box I wanted to keep for myself. I told him that I couldn't find any box of fountain pens in his hospital room. He said that he had picked them up when he was in his office. Then he said things that showed he was confused about both what day it was and what time of day it was. He also told me to put the lower bed rail down so that after I left he could get up, use the bathroom and brush his teeth. I reminded him that he couldn't do it without his Nurse present. I didn't even state the fact that he isn't able to sit without help, much less stand and walk. I have no idea where this is coming from, or what it indicates. I will absolutely ask them at HUP next week.

So the days tick by and he progresses. Clearly, it's not any more of a straight line up than it was at HUP.

xxoo M'ree
Organ Donors Save Lives

∞

6/7/2007   Not Much New

When I was wheeling Jeff from gym PT to the dining room OT yesterday, there were three men in the main hall with their therapy dogs. The first one, Timmy, was an older black mixed breed, with a very white muzzle. When Jeff said his name, he went right over and sat down next to the wheelchair so Jeff could pet him. The second one was a white poodle mix, unclipped. I forget her name, but she was very cute and very sweet. The last one was a yellow golden retriever, who licked Jeff's hand and arm all over. I don't remember his name, either. The dogs just sucked up all the attention and their masters were very friendly and cheery, too. What a great perk! I didn't ask how often they come in.

Today I didn't see any therapy. Jeff was in bed, very soundly asleep, when I arrived. He had both a chest x-ray and a long

PT session in the morning. He never did stand, because it turns out that the available frame didn't have knee braces and he's not strong enough yet to stand without those. The afternoon was supposed to consist of more Speech/Swallow therapy and a short PT session. The Speech/Swallow Therapist got delayed and didn't come. When the PT Therapists arrived, Jeff had a bout of the runs and the time ran out before they could get him cleaned up. They did say that he was making good progress overall and definitely getting stronger. Anyway, he promptly fell asleep again and woke briefly while our friend, Sue, visited. She told her usual great stories that made him laugh.

The best news is that he was not confused and he was in a good mood. He said that his chest pain was almost gone and his stomach was fine. He's not as gurgly in the throat as he has been, either. That's really good, because it indicates that he's dealing with his secretions by swallowing and is closer to eating by mouth. He keeps saying that he wants two things: to eat, and to go home. In that order.

xxoo M'ree
Organ Donors Save Lives

∞

6/9/2007   Reading

Today I also missed Jeff's therapy sessions. He didn't stand, again because the frame was being used, but he did a lot of the sitting bicycle, which will go a long way to strengthening his legs. He also did work with the arm dowels. He also had sessions with both Speech/Swallow and Psychology, but I don't know what happened there. The PT and OT Therapists tell me he is making good progress.

He sat in the wheelchair all afternoon, which was a change from the past couple of days. He produced a ton of lung secretions while sitting. My sense is that his upper body had a big workout throughout the day. Since he was awake and alert, I would have loved to have taken him outside for a walk, but it was 95 degrees and very humid. The weekend should be cooler and less humid, so maybe I can talk him into it then. For the second day, he wanted me to read to him from my latest book, Viktor Frankl's "Man's Search for Meaning", which was recommended to me by my friend, Annamaria. Sometimes he asks me to re-read passages. We are both riveted.

His spirits were great. Jeff is definitely feeling more positive and in control of things generally. He talks a lot about going home and unquestionably believes he WILL get there. At last!

xxoo M'ree
Organ Donors Save Lives

∞

6/9/2007   Bed Transplant

The biggest news today is that we've had a bed transplant at home. Our bed is waist-tall to me. The bed itself is a regular bed, the mattress is a very thick latex foam model, and the traditional box spring has been replaced by a wooden box that Jeff built and I upholstered. I've been fretting about whether, and how, Jeff would get into that high bed. Now that he could possibly be home within a few weeks, I decided it was time for action. Our friend, Galen, who builds furniture and has renovated old houses, came over yesterday, uncovered and disassembled the box, took it home and cut it down. This morning, he brought it back, reassembled it, recovered it, and now it's at a more normal height. Piece of cake. Well, not exactly, but Galen made it seem easy. Now I can stop fretting about that. Thank you so much, Galen!

There was only a little therapy today, because it's the weekend. He used the hand bicycle in OT this afternoon. He helps to get himself from bed into the wheelchair to a reasonable degree now and he can scoot himself into the back of the chair seat. Neither I nor his Nurse can fathom why they scheduled another OT session from 6:30 - 7pm. Maybe they will do something in his room. I'll find out tomorrow.

His ascites has increased to the point that he has a big belly again. That holds him back to some extent with his therapy because it makes him short of wind, not to mention the extra weight to move around plus the fact that he can't bend much or easily. They are debating what to do about it. I'm sure they will get some input from HUP on Tuesday after his appointment there. I do miss having the almost daily interaction with the doctors. That doesn't happen at BMR.

Today Jeff was in very good spirits again. I'm thinking that he's about out of the deepest depths of the emotional pit, at least for now. He asked me to take him to the Horticulture Therapy wing on the first floor (it's like a big greenhouse) which he can see from the OT windows. After his OT, I wheeled him downstairs, only to find that wing is closed and locked on the weekends. He can look forward to doing that one-day next week. So I wheeled him around the entire first floor. It's very interesting, because the walls are lined with gorgeous original art work that is all done by people who have disabilities. Good distraction and inspiration, too.

xxoo M'ree
Organ Donors Save Lives

6/10/2007 Slow Sunday

Today Jeff had an hour of PT before I arrived, but I wasn't able to find out anything about what or how he did. He would only tell me that he did exercises. He didn't remember whether he stood or not. While I was there, he had a half-hour of Speech Therapy. The Therapist asked him to read a few short paragraphs, and then answer questions about the content. He passed with flying colors. No issues there. I asked her when they would give him another swallow test. She thought very soon: probably this week.

Jeff wasn't feeling very well generally today and was nauseous during the afternoon. There doesn't seem to be a specific reason, and he's not ill, so we just roll with it. He was also a little confused. He asked me if I found the wadded up $20 bill when I made his bed. He also told me that he had been home a couple of days ago and packed some handkerchiefs when he returned to HUP. He also said that he would walk me to the elevator when I was ready to go. That stuff always throws me for a loop. I'll mention it to the HUP teams on Tuesday and see what they say about it. My guess is that it's related to his meds.

xxoo M'ree
Organ Donors Save Lives

∞

6/11/2007   Could It Be He's Back at HUP?

Yes, folks, it surely could. The phone startled me awake at 1:30am. A doctor from BMR gave me his name, but I didn't write it down and now I can't remember it. He said that he actually works at HUP and was on assignment at BMR. He said that Jeff's ascites and edema were concerning them enough that they were sending him to HUP for a look-see. They felt that they should send him right away rather than wait until the morning, because they know how badly the ER fills up at daylight. The doctor told me to go back to bed and get some sleep. Right.

So I called HUP at 6am. He was still in the ER. They

wouldn't tell me much over the phone (privacy issues, even though I'm Jeff's wife) but they did tell me that he was there, they were waiting for test results, and that they had not made a decision as to whether to admit him. I should call back later. I called again at 9:30 and got to speak with his Attending, who told me that they were going to admit Jeff, but didn't have a bed yet. I told him that I was on my way.

Jeff seemed fine in the sense that he was calm, but he was mentally confused; more so than yesterday. I sat with Jeff in the ER all day. One of the original Transplant Team Doctors came by and said that the plan is to keep him there for "a few days" until they can get his fluids under control. Then they will send him back to BMR. The Doctor asked him a few questions to check his mental status, all of which he answered correctly. The Doctor commented that he hadn't ever heard Jeff's voice because he left for vacation before they removed the trach.

By 6:30pm, the bed they had assigned to Jeff still hadn't been vacated. It's supposed to be just down the hall from where he was before. They expected to be able to move him in a few hours. Jeff was sleeping soundly, so I decided to go home. I woke him first so he would know I was leaving.

Tomorrow I'll have to call BMR to see if they want me to pick up Jeff's stuff. I have no idea how long they can hold his room empty. Also, they didn't send his eyeglasses with him, so he'll be blind. So it seems to me that I'll be on the road tomorrow to fetch them.

It's always something.

xxoo M'ree
Organ Donors Save Lives

6/12/2007   Assessment Day

The most important news comes first: Jeff is not experiencing any rejection. His ascites and edema have gotten beyond acceptable limits. The HUP team has decided not to tap his belly; they are going to remove the fluids with drugs, which they have already started. The Transplant Team Head rounded with the others and said that when someone has the degree of liver disease that Jeff had, these things sometimes happen during recovery and they are not concerned about it. He thinks that after about two days, Jeff will be ok to return to BMR. Ah, the relief!

Jeff got to his room after 10pm yesterday. Today, when I arrived, the PT team had just entered his room. They want to be sure he doesn't lose any ground while he's at HUP. They tested his leg and arm strength, and were very impressed. They had him sit up on the edge of the bed for a while. Jeff did fine. They are coming back tomorrow. It will be so much easier for Jeff when that fluid is gone, even a little.

During the day, there were the usual tests: chest x-ray, lots of blood draws, etc. They started TPN nutrition via the Peg Tube.

When the word spread that Jeff was back, HUP visitors started showing up. Nurses who had cared for him, the Physical Therapist he called a "lying devil" when she kept him standing for longer than she promised, the Social Worker, etc. Everyone said how often they think about Jeff and how much healthier and stronger he seems. They love his southern accent, which they hadn't heard before. The Social Worker asked whether he is eating by mouth. When I told her that BMR intended to try another speech/swallow test soon, I thought to ask her if it would be possible to have one done at HUP. She ran out to make the request. It's set for tomorrow. Yesssssssssss!

Before I left the house today, I called BMR. I wanted to get his glasses, which they had neglected to send with him. Not only had they already packed up his stuff and put it into storage, there is another patient in "his" room. Who knows whether he will get the same room when he returns, or another one? Not that it matters.

So, anyway, we can all relax now. I'm going to relax big time right starting this very minute.

xxoo M'ree
Organ Donors Save Lives

∞

6/13/2007   Moving Back Tomorrow

Great news! Jeff's fluid reduction is progressing well with the meds they are using, so the Transplant Team Head said they will continue that program. He will be pleased if the issue resolves within about a week. So Jeff is scheduled to be picked up at 10am tomorrow to go back to BMR. I'm going to call HUP before I drive to BMR, just to be sure. They promised they would remember to send his eyeglasses with him.

Even greater news: Jeff passed the swallow test today! This means they can start giving him small amounts of applesauce, pudding, and the like, in addition to his tube feeds. He must be sitting at 90°, and he must swallow two or three times after each spoonful. Before the test, he was very agitated, and he tried to distract the Therapist by saying that his legs hurt, then his back hurt, etc. He finally admitted, tearfully, that he was afraid he wouldn't be able to keep food down. If I'd had even an inkling that he was thinking that way, I would have tried to head it off in advance. The Therapist calmly explained that his tube feeds have been going into his stomach, so that's not an issue. He relaxed after that. This just demonstrates to me that none of us have a clue what is going on in his head. I'm going to try my best to encourage him to talk to me as much as possible. He's not much into talking.

There was no PT today, but that's not unusual.

He is totally bored at HUP. I'm sure he is now used to all the therapy sessions and the people interaction that goes with it. He's very ready to move ahead.

Lastly, our Pennsylvania "Organ Donor" automobile license plate finally arrived today, after an almost five-month wait. It has an emblem saying "Donate Life" on the left side, and the words "Organ Donors Save Lives" across the bottom. If it encourages even one person to sign up, the $22.50 investment will have been repaid a trillion fold.

xxoo M'ree
Organ Donors Save Lives

∞

6/14/2007   Back at BMR

It's done. He's moved back, and into the same room. I just had to unpack all his stuff and hang everything back on the walls. Now they have to re-evaluate him in every respect, including swallowing, because they won't take HUP's word for any of it. That will all happen tomorrow. Then he'll start therapy again.

I'd say that he's glad to be back, but the days of inactivity at HUP have clearly taken their toll emotionally. His personality is as flat as a pancake. Not crying or hostile, but absolutely flat, and, I'm sure, very fragile. He said he is tired. I'm hoping like heck that tomorrow will pick him up, even if it's only a little. Team of Angels, give him a little energy and encouragement, would you, please?

xxoo M'ree
Organ Donors Save Lives

∞

6/15/2007   Nary a Skipped Beat

Today was another Assessment Day. Before I arrived, he
had Speech/Swallow, Psychology, PT and OT. I asked him
if Speech/Swallow did another test and he said they just asked him
questions. The only therapist I got to speak with was PT; I don't
know exactly what happened in any of the other sessions.

While I was there, he had more PT and more OT. The
Physical Therapist said that they didn't have him stand in the
morning, but he hasn't lost any ground from their perspective. She
had him rolling onto his side, sitting on the edge of the bed, and
transferring into the wheelchair. He sat there for over an hour until it
was time for OT. The Occupational Therapist had him do lots of
general cardiovascular arm exercises, plus some arm strengthening
exercises. He did very well, especially after a whole day of effort.

He seems sad, but it was easy for everyone to get him
smiling. He's discouraged about how long his recovery is taking. He
knows that Christy and Robin may be coming in July, and he's upset
that he may still be at BMR. He so wants to get out of bed by
himself. I think of that as the next big milestone. I must noodle how
to get him more focused on what he CAN do now.

His edema is much improved, and his ascites is lessening.

Better living through chemistry.

They were going to give him a shower before they put him back into bed for the night. Sounds like a good plan for me, too, but I'll substitute a long soak. This has been a very long week.

xxoo M'ree
Organ Donors Save Lives

∞

6/16/2007 Tell Me Why

Why is Jeff's voice so soft? He talks, but it's as if he is too weak to make himself heard. I don't believe it's depression. He's not sick at all. Maybe his muscles are sore from all those upper body exercises, and it makes it hard for him to force the air out. It's likely to be Monday before I see the Speech/Swallow Therapist to ask. Darned if I can figure it out.

And why has he gotten into the habit of talking to people without looking at them? When I talk to him, I actually say, "Jeff, look at me." Then he does. I'm going to ask about that, too.

Enough questions.

Today started with an hour of PT in the downstairs gym. The Therapist told me that he stood up. She said he had lots of help from two people, and he only stood for about five seconds, but he stood with parallel bars; no standing frame. Wow! They would have continued, but he had a severe diarrhea episode (if you asked my opinion, I'd guess it was from nerves), and they had to take him back to the room for cleanup. Then he had an hour of OT in his room, including lots of arm exercises. I arrived in the middle of that. Then another hour of PT in his room, for lots of leg exercises. He tolerated it all well and in good humor.

Then our friends, Galen and Margaret, visited for a long time. Unfortunately, Jeff was exhausted from the therapy and slept most of the time. You know how "they" say that people in a coma hear what people say in their presence? Well, I do believe that, on some level, Jeff was participating in his sleep. If so, he enjoyed himself as much as I did.

My personal goal for next week is to meet with his Case Manager to get more info about his progress, his goals for discharge, what may happen after that (maybe outpatient visits?), etc. I think he's been there long enough for them to give me some idea, even though he did go back to HUP for a few days.

xxoo M'ree
Organ Donors Save Lives

∞

6/17/2007   Very Interesting

Today was much better than yesterday, at least, from my perspective. The Father's Day cards and phone calls cheered him, for sure. My brother, Joe, and his wife, Eileen, visited, too, after a family wedding. We don't see them often enough, so any reason is fine.

Then there was the therapy dog, Gina, who came in dressed like a man, complete with shirt and tie. She was a lab mix, old and very sweet. The people who do that with their dogs are so special.

He had PT for half an hour, so I made sure we had him dressed and into the wheelchair in advance, so I could get him there on time. The Therapist was about five feet tall and extremely petite overall and she had an assistant working with her. She told Jeff she wanted him to stand up using a walker with a table-top attachment. First Jeff said he was too weak, then he was too tired, then she was too small and he would hurt her, then she was not strong enough to hold him up, then the walker was not sturdy enough, then he cried and said that he was scared to death that he would fall flat on his face. She listened, said she understood, and then she firmly asked if he would rather use the walker or a folding ladder. He said he would use the walker. Then he stood up. He had a lot of help, but he did it. During the brief process, he was insisting he couldn't do it. The Therapist just said his name and gave him clear instructions, which he followed. I was standing in front of him. He looked me in the eye and mouthed a kiss. Then he sat back down. Then she made a fist at him and said that if he ever told her she was too small again she would pop him. That made him laugh. Overall, it was a major achievement in my view. I'm sure they will stand him up every day.

His voice was stronger all day. He keeps talking negatively: can't do this, won't be able to do that, etc., and I keep responding that he needs to be positive, and I remind him about when he really couldn't do anything and all the things he can do now, plus what he will be doing very soon. I'm just not going to let him wallow in "woe is me" mode. Period.

xxoo M'ree
Organ Donors Save Lives

∞

6/18/2007   Positive Direction

Today was even better than yesterday. Jeff had a total of three hours of PT plus three hours of OT plus 1/2 hour of Speech/Swallow. I was only there for one hour of PT and the Speech/Swallow. He still has the runs. They have tested him again for bacteria to see if they should give him any other drugs. This seems to be a cyclical event.

Physically, he's making serious progress in small steps. In my presence, he stood three times, but he only got completely up once and only for a few seconds. He said his left knee, which had surgery before TJ was born, was giving out. He fussed a teeny bit, but his fear is almost totally gone. I do believe that he finally believes he can and will stand on his own.

He also ate 10 teeny swallows of applesauce without a hitch; of course, he said it wasn't as good as the Mott's brand he loves. He is scheduled to go to Paoli Hospital on Thursday afternoon for a swallow study (a "fluoroscopy") using barium. The gist of it is that they mix an assortment of different foods with a little barium to watch exactly where it goes when he swallows. The Therapist does not think they will find any issues, but they do it to be absolutely certain that they can start regular food without aspiration danger. I can go along, but I can't be present in the x-ray room during the test itself.

When I think of how far he's come in not very a long time, I'm so happy and grateful. I think I'll celebrate with a whirlpool bath.

xxoo M'ree
Organ Donors Save Lives

∞

6/19/2007   Severe Thunder Storms

...are coming soon, so I'm going to type as fast as I can to get offline before they hit.

Lots of things today. First, Jeff's spirits are good, even though he's uncomfortable physically. A GI Doctor from Paoli Hospital stopped by to tell me that his gastric issues are not due to bacteria, but to a strong antibiotic he's taking. They are now giving him another drug to lessen that side effect. She also told me that BMR is working closely with the HUP Transplant Team to keep his fluids, etc. under control. They are exchanging info daily and will adjust the meds as needed. He will have another visit to HUP in two weeks.

Also, the Case Manager spent some time with me. After the pow-wow today, the word is that they still expect him to be there for four to six weeks. She said he didn't lose any ground by being back at HUP for a few days, but he didn't make any progress, either. They can't predict with any degree of certainty exactly what he will be able to do when he comes home. The goal is to have him out of a wheelchair, but he may not be completely there. He should be advanced enough that I can care for him without full-time help. He will surely need some out-patient visits, at least. I wouldn't have expected any different.

Today he ate more applesauce and had both OT and PT. He stood again twice, each time for over a minute, at the parallel bars in the big, first floor gym. He showed no fear. His left knee is giving him a fit because his muscles aren't strong enough to take the brunt of the work. Each time, he had to sit because his knee was giving out. It was just wonderful to see him stand and looking fairly relaxed. The effort wiped him out totally, and he went right to sleep afterwards.

I want more days like this.

xxoo M'ree
Organ Donors Save Lives

∞

6/20/2007   Great Strides

Today Jeff made a lot of progress. When I went to PT with

him, his usual gregarious personality had returned and he had the Therapist and helpers laughing. That alone thrilled me. Then he stood twice, each time for over two minutes, and with minimal help after he got up. The Psychologist co-treated and gave him good hints, e.g., imagining himself standing in our kitchen, breathing deeply and not feeling anxious. While he was standing, he chatted about cutting up veggies for soup, etc. It was just wonderful. And, best of all, this was after a full morning of PT and OT, including more standing.

The next OT goal is to get him strong enough to hoist himself to a standing position and stand up by himself, so he could, for example, stand at the sink to brush his teeth. There's a good example of the difference between OT and PT. OT is concerned with daily living activities; PT is concerned with physical ability.

Jeff's edema and ascites are lessening. The gastric issues are stopping, too. It seems that his meds are working well together, at least, for the moment. There have been so many ups and downs that I have learned that nothing is forever.

He had applesauce again this morning. Tomorrow we both go to Paoli Hospital for the barium fluoroscopy to check his swallow mechanics. If that goes ok, he will start eating. I'm trying not to be too confident, just in case something goes goofy.

When he was finally back in bed and going to sleep, he said he was tired, but that he felt good. Music, absolute music, to my ears.

Oh, the storms last night were strong, but not extreme. No damages.

xxoo M'ree
Organ Donors Save Lives

∞

6/21/2007   Honey Foul

Well, the barium fluoroscopy went fine with both applesauce and peaches. When they tried with honey, he aspirated. We won't know the impact of that outcome until tomorrow when the Speech/Swallow Therapist lets us know. The technician said that he had a great deal of secretions in his throat, which would have impacted his ability to swallow. I don't know if the fact that he was extremely nervous had anything to do with it. No matter. He will swallow perfectly when he's perfectly ready to swallow perfectly. When we returned to BMR, he said he was concerned that he wouldn't be able to eat soon. I told him that I had already asked the Case Manager about the subject, and that tube feeds do not have to be discontinued before he is discharged. That made him relax, at least enough to fall asleep right away.

In the morning, before he went for the swallow test, he had 1 1/2 hours each of PT and OT. He stood again, twice, for more than two minutes. He's getting pretty confident about his ability. He's also helping much more to "transfer", which is what they call it when he moves, say, from bed to wheelchair. He can also roll from side to side in bed pretty easily now.

The Psychologist came in after he was back in bed and talked to him for a while about his general nervousness. She gave him breathing exercises to do any time, including while he's standing. She also told him that she's instructing the Therapists to *tell* him what they want him to do, rather than *ask* him what he wants to do. She said he is underestimating his ability. He agreed and said that would be fine with him. From what I've observed, that's an excellent approach.

Last night our friends, John and Penny, visited him for a long time. They said that he was his old self and that he was in a great mood. That made me feel so good. Sometimes I wonder if he gets down in the evenings after I leave.

Today is our fifth wedding anniversary. That sneaky snake had the Psychologist get a card for him to give me. Can you imagine? I was speechless and so deeply touched. We made a date to spend our next anniversary on Monhegan Island, which was the scene of the crime. Amen.

xxoo M'ree
Organ Donors Save Lives

∞

6/22/2007 Frustrated

That's me today, because the Speech/Swallow Therapist didn't see Jeff, so we know nothing about the feeding plan. I'm sure we won't learn anything over the weekend, so we must be patient (no pun intended). Jeff, on the other hand, doesn't seem to care. Thank goodness.

Otherwise, the day was totally uneventful. More PT and OT. No standing, because Jeff was too tired. We did go outside between therapy sessions. It was glorious to feel the breeze.

Wish there was more to report. Probably not over the weekend, either.

xxoo M'ree
Organ Donors Save Lives

∞

6/23/2007 Administrative Decision

Ok, it's that time. I was beginning to think it would never come. This is a day of nothing to say, because it was just OT and resting. I've decided that from now on, if there is anything of note, I'll write. Otherwise, I won't write.

xxoo M'ree
Organ Donors Save Lives

∞

6/26/2007   First Lunch?

Back again with a bunch of news.

When I arrived today, there was one of those hospital lunch order lists sitting on Jeff's table. And there was the usual daily schedule, which showed that he had a Speech/Swallow therapy session scheduled during lunch. So here's his first lunch menu: thick pureed fruit blend; thick pureed beef, macaroni and tomato casserole; thick pureed green beans; and applesauce. Yummmm! Hey, I shouldn't make fun. He said it felt strange to eat, but that it wasn't bad. I don't know how much volume he ate, but he did it and didn't aspirate. I also don't know if they plan to re-do the barium fluoroscopy. I'll ask the next time I get to see the Therapist.

Now to his left knee. He has been complaining that it hurts, but he did have surgery on it some 38 years ago, and it sometimes flares up when he overdoes it. Also, at some point way in the past, a doctor told him that he's likely to need a knee replacement "sometime" and that's in the back of his mind. Well, yesterday when he woke up, the knee was pretty swollen and hot, not red, though. So they did an x-ray right away and didn't try any standing yesterday. This morning they said the x-ray showed arthritis, but that he could stand if he could tolerate the pain. So he stood during PT. And they scheduled a Thursday morning trip to Paoli hospital to see an orthopod. They said that they may either aspirate some of the accumulated fluid or recommend a steroid shot. Jeff doesn't like the idea of steroids, so we'll see what happens. As long as they aren't saying he needs a knee replacement right now. Oh, please, not that, too!

He has a motorized wheelchair now, and is doing a really good job of maneuvering it, slowly, around the halls. They have even practiced getting in and out of the elevator with it. That's much more freedom and autonomy for him, even though he can't get in and out of it by himself. He likes it.

He is also admitting to anxiety about coming home: he mentioned both worry about needing to use the bathroom in the middle of the night, and also fear of falling out of the wheelchair. Mind you, we have no idea whether he will, in fact, come home with a wheelchair. He's just spending his leisure time imagining being back at home and worrying about what it will be like. Everyone is doing a great job of listening to and acknowledging his fears and then calmly and rationally helping to dispel them. It must be absolutely overwhelming to think about returning to relatively total autonomy after complete dependence for such a long time. The Psychologist did ask him if he would be willing to take meds for his mood, and he said an emphatic NO. Today his mood was very positive and he was talkative and joking with everyone.

xxoo M'ree
Organ Donors Save Lives

7/1/2007   Saturday Shuffle

Yesterday Jeff greeted me with a big smile and a "Guess what I did this morning?" He walked! Well, he said it was really more of a shuffle, because he said it was difficult to actually lift his feet off the ground. He was in the downstairs gym, standing between the parallel bars, with one big guy in front of him and one behind. He said he walked from one end of the bars to the other. I'd say that's about 15 feet or so. Now, I didn't witness it, but he was just pleased as could be about it. I did a little dance, myself. I hope to see him do it soon.

Late in the week, I attended a PT session where Jeff stood up (with a little help from two Therapists) from his wheelchair while holding onto a bar on the wall. This was a first, and he did it three times. Also, he can now raise himself up to a sitting position in his bed. He's really gaining strength fast now, which is huge progress.

About his knee: I met him at the orthopod's office on Thursday morning. He was so worked up about going that he said he tossed his cookies while getting onto the gurney. The Doctor was great interpersonally and was very calming. He showed us the x-rays that prove arthritis. He explained about aspirating the fluid which would make him more comfortable immediately. Then he explained about the purpose of and expected results from the steroid injection. Jeff said ok. It was all over in about 5 minutes, with no pain. Then the Doctor asked Jeff to bend his knee. Jeff teared up and said he was afraid, but then he just bent his leg and said that it felt pretty good and gave us a big smile. Deed done. Now he says it still feels much improved. Just what we wanted.

I also got to attend a Speech/Swallow session. The Therapist said that at some point down the road, they will likely repeat the barium fluoroscopy. The one they did showed that Jeff's throat muscles are still a little weak. They work most of the time, but not always. She gave him four specific exercises to strengthen the muscles. In addition to that, she will continue to give him pureed food regularly to help with the process. She told me that since Jeff has very clear food preferences, I could bring flavored instant oatmeal, cinnamon applesauce, and canned fruit that I puree. So now he has a stock in the fridge and in his closet. Sorbet will have to wait, because it totally liquefies in the mouth. He said that he is hungry. Since he's getting total nutrition from his tube feeds, I think it's not actual hunger, but more thinking about food. He said he's craving liver (of all things) and onions from Ray's Diner not far from our house. All this stimulates him do the exercises. Good!

This is a month since he arrived at BMR, except for the days he was back at HUP. I'm very encouraged by his progress. He still gets down sometimes when he thinks about how long he has been in HUP, or about the people he misses from his old job, or about what he can't do now, or about what he is afraid he won't be able to do when he comes home. No doubt it will be a tremendous adjustment for both of us, but we will be OK.

xxoo M'ree
Organ Donors Save Lives

∞

7/4/2007   Walkies

He's really walking now! His first stroll was on June 30th, one month to the day after he arrived at BMR. He had been standing at the parallel bars for a few minutes, having had a reasonable amount of help to get up from a sitting position. Two Therapists were working with him and he said he wanted to walk. And he did! Now he's walking a few times every day, more naturally, both between the parallel bars and also with a rolling stand that comes up to his waist and has a padded armrest with handles so he has more support than with a traditional walker.

And - this is fun - he now has an electric, reclining wheelchair so he can drive himself around. We even go for "walks" outside. He's operating it really well and gets on and off the elevator himself. He can't get into or out of the chair without help yet. He still needs some help to sit up from a horizontal position and to stand from a sitting position. They are doing a lot of strengthening work, so maybe it won't be too long.

They did an x-ray type swallowing test to check his throat muscles. They aren't strong enough yet to eat normally, so he still gets his nourishment via tube into his stomach, but Therapists give him pureed foods during supervised trials. He's doing fine with that.

In time, they will start giving him more normally-textured foods. Then, when they are confident that he can get total nourishment via mouth, they will slowly discontinue the tube feeds. When they are positive he won't need it again, they will remove the tube.

As of yesterday, he weighs 179 pounds, still a lot lower than his healthy 205, but a huge gain from where he was after the transplant. Wouldn't it be super if I could give him some of the pounds I've gained by overeating since he's been in HUP?

His new liver is still working perfectly, as it has done from day one. We will always be grateful for his donor's gift of life.

More news as it happens. Keep smiling!

xxoo M'ree
Organ Donors Save Lives

∞

7/4/2007   Walkies and Factoids

You should see him walking now! He's walking a few times every day, more naturally, both between the parallel bars and also with the rolling stand. He looks relaxed and comfortable. His fear is totally gone. It's just wonderful.

He seems to have gotten over a big emotional hump all of a sudden. He asks to go outside, which used to bum him out for whatever reason; he could never explain why. His personality is back. He talks to other patients and to people in the halls. He likes to do his exercises and asks for more until he's really tired.

The one thing he really, really wants is to eat. Yesterday he ate the pureed peaches with gusto. He still sounds a little gurgly when he swallows, but his throat is getting stronger.

Yesterday morning, he had a follow-up appointment at HUP. We were seen by one of the GI Doctors. We learned a few things: Jeff now weighs 179 pounds (he stood up on their scale). The immuno-suppressant drug he's taking probably contributed substantially to the post-surgical buildup of ascites fluid. They changed the dose and now his belly is way down. Another drug he's taking has probably caused his chronic diarrhea. They are changing that one, too.

Lastly, I never knew before today, but his MELD score (Model End-stage Liver Disease score, which indicates how poorly the liver is functioning) the day before transplant was 33. The scale tops out at 40.

His new liver is still working perfectly, as it has done from day one. We will always be grateful for his donor's gift of life.

xxoo M'ree
Organ Donors Save Lives

∞

7/11/2007   Got a Crystal Ball?

Jeff must have missed everyone at HUP a lot, because he

went back today. He woke up with a fever and nausea, complaining of belly pain and tenderness. Rather than make him lie in the HUP ER all day, they just admitted him. They are doing tests to figure out what's going on and will treat whatever it is. The goal is to get him back to BMR as soon as possible.

Over the past few days at BMR, he has continued to get stronger. Yesterday he walked three times (with the walker) for a total of 150 feet. This is just 10 days from not being able to take even one step. He's standing regularly, with support, and gets up fairly easily from a sitting position. He's sitting very well, but still needs help getting from a horizontal position to a sitting position. Despite this progress, he has complained of belly pain over the past few days, which the staff attributed to anxiety about beginning to eat pureed foods. He has also been more down in the dumps and crabby. Now it seems that he was actually getting sick. Oh, boy, this is a delicate balancing act. We don't want him to suffer, of course, but we also don't want him to malinger. How do we tell the difference? We sure could use a crystal ball.

xxoo M'ree
Organ Donors Save Lives

7/14/2007   Alarm Cancelled

He's back at BMR as of yesterday. Same room again. No liver rejection. No peritonitis. Fever is down, but he still has some belly pain. They don't yet have all the various culture results, but whatever it was, it's resolving with the antibiotics they are giving him. Oh, boy!

One very interesting thing was told to us by a HUP Doctor - the one who is their King of Deconditioning. He told us the rule of thumb is that for every deconditioned day a patient has, it will take two rehab days to recover. Let's see: Jeff was inpatient at HUP from February 16th through May 30th. That's 104 days. Which would mean 208 rehab days. I'm praying most of that will be at home.

xxoo M'ree
Organ Donors Save Lives

∞

7/27/2007   TENTATIVE Discharge Date

It looks as if Jeff's hospital days are numbered. The BMR Case Manager told me yesterday that they are targeting Saturday, August 4th, as his discharge date. Make no mistake: even if it happens, it's far from the end of the journey. He will come home with a lot of gear, including a wheelchair, walker, maybe a hospital bed, etc., etc. He will also have regular home visits for therapy, nursing, etc. In addition, we will have a Certified Home Health Aide ("CHHA") daily during the week for the time being so he will have care while I work. Insurance will cover everything except for the CHHA, which won't come cheap. Here's where his disability insurance will be a life-saver. Long ago we did apply for Long Term

Care insurance for both of us. They took me, but wouldn't sell Jeff the coverage because he had a liver condition. Of course. It reminded me that many years ago, when discussing the need for life and long term care insurance, my accountant said to me, "If you don't have kids, nobody cares if you die. God forbid you live."

Jeff is still being fed via gastric tube. He continues to have a fair amount of difficulty swallowing. They are continuing to work on it, but it's going very slowly and he's not excited by the pureed food they give him. Maybe my tasty homemade food will get a better result.

His progress with the other physical abilities is also very slow. He has trouble getting himself to a sitting position from lying down; usually he needs help. His standing from a seated position is getting easier little by little. He is still walking with a walker, but can't go very far. Yesterday, for the first time, he climbed six four-inch high steps, and went down forwards, too. He did it very smoothly, but as you would expect, his stamina is virtually nil. He can slowly move his own wheelchair on level ground.

From a health perspective, Jeff's liver is still perfect. He has a good bit of ascites, but his edema is gone. He still has periodic bouts of not feeling well, including stomach and gastric upset, probably due in large part to the meds. He still has an effusion in one of his lungs, so he has a fair amount of secretions. I sure wish he felt better overall.

He has finally admitted to himself that he's depressed, and agreed to take meds. They started this week, so we should begin to see improvement soon. We all believe that this will go a long way to helping him improve.

So I'm trying to prepare for the next stage of our lives and wondering what it will be like. The critical issues are: keeping up with his therapy and exercise so he doesn't slip back or get pneumonia; getting him to oral nutrition; watching his health; and building his stamina. It's more than a little daunting, I admit, but we can handle it. Jeff is very afraid. Other than listening and reassurance, which everyone is giving him, he has to just do it. I'm calling on that Team of Angels to give strength to both of us.

xxoo M'ree
Organ Donors Save Lives

∞

8/2/2007   How Spooky is This?

Last night I was pretty anxious and finally fell asleep at about 10pm, with help from a Moon Drop, my homeopathic sleep potion. At 11pm I sat straight up in bed with my heart racing and thought I should call Jeff's Nurse. I rang the number and the tech answered. I told her I was calling to check on Jeff and she said that a doctor was in his room at that moment. Seems he started throwing up his tube feed and had a lot of diarrhea. His Nurse got the phone and said he was stable and didn't have a fever. She promised to have the doctor call me when he was done examining Jeff. About 15 minutes later the doctor called. Jeff was stable. They were set to restart the tube feed in about two hours at a lower rate. They will make a decision later about what to do. I said that since he's set to come home on Saturday and the doctors are also talking about his throat issue, it may be a good idea to send him to HUP. That made sense to the doctor. We'll see what happens.

In preparation for Jeff's discharge, the plumber/electrician is coming to the house tomorrow morning to install shower bars and a bedroom ceiling fan. My nephew, Lee and his strong buddy are coming in the evening to rearrange the bedroom furniture to accommodate a hospital bed, as well as the wheelchair and walker.

xxoo M'ree
Organ Donors Save Lives

∞

8/4/2007   From BMR to... Not Home

Yes, you read it right: not home. Jeff was transferred back to HUP yesterday, after a 48 hour wait for bed availability. It's not what we expected, but what's new?

There are a few things going on. The most straightforward is that he has an infection, complete with fever, nausea, etc. BMR had already put him on antibiotics. HUP will certainly figure out what's up with that and fix it. Next is that he has pleural effusions. In plain English, this means that fluid has accumulated in the chest around the lungs. Since the transplant, he's had an effusion on one side, but now it's both. That does not seem to be concerning anyone to any great degree; they just mentioned it to me. I have no idea what they will do about that, if anything. Also, his ascites seems to be increasing slightly. If past experience is a predictor of the future, they will just change and/or increase his diuretics to handle that.

The biggest issue is eating by mouth. The BMR Speech/Swallow Therapist and their GI Doctor have concluded that there must be something physical going on between his throat and his stomach, so he's been back to "nothing by mouth" for a few days. When he swallows anything, it comes back up in about five minutes. Since he has no trouble keeping down his tube feeds, which go directly into his stomach, the stomach is not the problem. He is able to swallow, so it's not that part of his equipment. The issue could be as simple as an overgrowth of candida (like thrush in a baby's mouth), or as complex as some sort of stricture somewhere. The only way to make a definite diagnosis is to put a scope down his throat and take a look. BMR is not equipped to do that. The very best news is that since it's a GI issue, Jeff's long-time and favorite GI Doctor, the original PCP, who treated him up until the transplant, is now the main man. Go, go, go!

If you asked me, I'd say the depression med is starting to kick in, because he's not nearly as down these days.

So all plans to bring him home are on hold. The house is ready for his arrival: horizontal and vertical grab bars have been installed in the shower; the bedroom furniture has been rearranged to accommodate a hospital bed; we have his wheelchair and walker; I have tons of other stuff for his care. Delivery of the bed and the other equipment has been postponed. Bayada Nursing is waiting for an update.

xxoo M'ree
Organ Donors Save Lives

8/14/2007   You'll Believe This for Sure

...because there's no way I could be making all this up. Let me say straight off that the news is not that bad, but it's just so bizarre.

Jeff has returned to HUP and will be here for an unknown duration. He was actually admitted as a liver (medicine, not transplant) patient, rather than GI. This means that his old PCP is not his Attending Physician, but he has been around to visit. No matter; we're ok with that.

Here's a laundry list of issues:

- Pneumonia in his left lung, diagnosed on the day after he arrived. Being treated with antibiotics and resolving nicely. Waiting for another x-ray to determine if it's totally gone.

- An ileus (read: area in the intestine where stuff is not moving through like it should), diagnosed on the day after he arrived.

Resolved by itself.

- C-diff bacteria in his intestines, diagnosed before he left BMR. Resolved with antibiotics.

- Ascites that is worse again, but this time it's not in one big abdominal area, but in many small pockets so they can't tap it. Being treated with diuretics and starting to lessen.

- Persistent nausea, caused by who-knows-what; likely due at least in part to one or a combination of meds he is on. This is preventing him from eating by mouth, since he can't keep anything down after he swallows it.

- Immunosuppressant level that is way too high. They think it's because one or a combination of meds has interfered with its metabolism. This has probably contributed to many of the above issues. It will take a while to resolve.

- The depression med has ceased having a positive effect, so they have switched to another drug, which does a few good things: stops nausea; increases appetite; encourages sleep; improves mood. All good for Jeff.

They did do tests to check his throat for physical problems. Result: There is no physical problem. Now once they get the nausea under control, they can start food by mouth again.

Now, are you ready for the kicker? On Sunday, I noticed that he had red bumps, some like blisters, equally distributed all over the

front and back of his body. By Monday, it was on his face, too. The
Dermatologists thought it was chicken pox, but no. Today the lab
proved that it's actually shingles, another manifestation of the same
varicella virus. It seems that when you get these diseases, they never
leave the body, but lie dormant in the spinal cord. Then, if you
become immunosuppressed, it can come back. Viola! For whatever
reason, it's not either painful or itching. Thank goodness, because he
doesn't need that discomfort, too. They are treating him with an
anti-viral. Because he's contagious as well as immuno-suppressed,
he's now in an isolation room, with the door always shut. It also has
"negative pressure", so no outside air goes either in or out of his
room. It does have two windows to the nurse's station, plus two
huge picture windows overlooking the Philadelphia skyline. Now, in
addition to gowns and gloves, anyone who goes in must also wear a
face mask. After all his bumps are dried up, he can go back to a
regular room.

The awful related complication comes because I don't know
whether I've ever had chicken pox. The only way to know is for me
to have a blood test to check for a "titer" (read: immunity). My PCP
can't draw my blood until Thursday, and the results won't be back for
about a week. Meanwhile, I've been exposed. If I have gotten the
virus, I'm contagious from "day 8 (the 8th day after Jeff's bumps
appeared = Sunday, August 19th) to day 21 (= Saturday, September
1st)". *I am now barred from Jeff's room until the earlier of a) when the lab says
I have a titer, or b) September 1st.* And, until then, I should avoid contact
with anyone who hasn't had chicken pox (maybe I should wear an

212

"unclean" sign?). So I said a temporary goodbye to Jeff before I left today. He took it ok. I will call Jeff's Nurse and Jeff regularly and hope he answers his phone.-

Physical Therapy has been working with him a little, and he's standing up again. He hasn't walked yet. Also, Speech/Swallow is working with him; today he had ice chips.

The Social Worker is trying her best, while all these balls are in the air, to figure out where he should go next; surely not home yet. There are a couple of possibilities, none of them BMR. He doesn't want to go back there and I just don't believe they are up to dealing with a medical case as complex as his.

I know he's in good hands with all the HUP doctors and nurses. Until I can be there again in person, the Team of Angels will have to fill in.

xxoo M'ree
Organ Donors Save Lives

∞

8/20/2007   You'll Believe This for Sure - Next Installment

The call came at 7:30am on Sunday. During the night he Jeff had trouble breathing. They did a CAT scan, which revealed a very large pleural effusion (fluid inside his chest cavity), which had collapsed his left lung. They immediately moved him to the ICU. They scared me, because they said they may have to intubate him again, which would be a huge setback.

Since then, they've determined that he does not have a clot and he does not have pneumonia, but they are giving him antibiotics just in case. They are being conservative, which pleases me. They have discussed a few treatments, but so far have only done a diagnostic thoracentesis (used a needle to take out about 60ccs of fluid for analysis). He's awake and relatively comfortable on oxygen. When they round today, which takes place anywhere from 10am to 1pm, they will figure out today's treatment plan and let me know.

His shingles is running its course. I'm hoping that the results of my blood test will be back maybe even today and that I have a titer, so I can go there. I'm SO frustrated. I won't let myself think that he's giving up the fight. Praying that both of us get strength.

xxoo M'ree
Organ Donors Save Lives

∞

8/22/2007   New Digs

Today HUP moved Jeff out of the ICU onto a regular medical floor.

My titer came back late on Monday; I'm immune to varicella, so I started going back to HUP on Tuesday.

Since Sunday, they have treated him very conservatively. They are still using an inflating vest that automatically vibrates to work the secretions out of his lungs. He hates it, but it works, so they insist, nicely. They have determined that there are no bacteria in his chest fluid and that he has no clots in his legs. He still does not have pneumonia. His effusions have reduced in size and his lungs are working fine with minimal oxygen. The shingles is resolving. His ascites is reduced. Thus the move.

The bad news is that his demeanor is very "flat", and he is sometimes confused. He looks pretty healthy, but he has absolutely lost ground physically and he has lost weight. His one remaining pressure ulcer has gotten a little larger. Also, as of yesterday, he has zero gag reflex, even if they stick the suction tube down his throat. They don't understand why and will be tackling this issue along with his nutrition. He can't take any food by mouth unless/until the gag reflex returns because he could easily aspirate. If you asked me whether he will be able to stand up when PT next visits, I'd say NO. Psych is on the way, too.

I'm worried about what is to come and how long it will take. I must put those thoughts out of my mind because it doesn't help anything for me to be upset. For distraction, I have a new project. I'm figuring out how to get him new tri-focal eyeglasses, because the ones he had at HUP never made it to the ICU when Jeff moved. I have looked everywhere at home for his old ones without success and Jeff can't remember where he put them. The place that I thought had made the current ones, about two years ago, says they didn't. Jeff can't remember who did. The place that made the previous ones in 2000 is willing to work with me. I can go there and pick out frames. They can wing it for the placement of the three sections; they said it would be worse to try a single vision version... They will teach me how to bend the ear pieces to fit at HUP. Then when Jeff finally gets out of there, he can have real ones made. Of course, as soon as I go through all this, HUP will find the lost ones.

Give me strength! And some sleep would be nice.

xxoo M'ree
Organ Donors Save Lives

∞

8/30/2007   He's Ready, Folks!

There's no sense in trying to figure it out. Jeff has turned yet another corner in just a few days. His health issues are almost completely resolved. His shingles are gone. His lungs and his chest are clear. He's not coughing up stuff. His ascites is almost gone. His edema is gone. His tube feeds have been much increased and he's tolerating them perfectly. His meds are fewer. The Physical and Occupational Therapists were there two days straight. Jeff is now standing with the walker (with help and not without effort, but he gets up and stays there) and yesterday he walked around the whole bed (slowly with the walker and with help). Mentally, he is almost completely back to himself. Today they are giving him one unit of blood because his hemoglobin is just under the acceptable limit. He has a ton of weight to gain. He still has no gag reflex so he can't start eating yet, but they assume this will come back in time. He still has that persistent pressure ulcer on his butt, but it's not any worse. He is absolutely ready for rehab again.

So our new Social Worker has seriously focused on getting the best for Jeff, and she succeeded big time today. Insurance approved another stint of acute rehab (like at BMR). Jeff does not want to go back to BMR for many reasons, but mostly because he simply has ultimate confidence in HUP. So the Social Worker lobbied big time for admission to the HUP rehab facility (The George Morris Piersol Rehabilitation Unit, called "Piersol" for short), and they have accepted him for admission tomorrow morning! This is an especially huge achievement because they only have 12 beds and they are very picky about whom they take, (they wouldn't take him last May because of his overall medical condition.) It's also very comforting because it's part of HUP so all Jeff's doctors are right there. If anything physical goes wrong, everyone and everything he needs is available. No more ambulance trips to other facilities where the doctors aren't familiar with his extraordinary case. And Jeff has total confidence in HUP, so he will be mentally at ease. And so will I.

So his bag of rehab clothes, etc., is re-packed and I'll take it tomorrow.

Hallelujah!

xxoo M'ree
Organ Donors Save Lives

∞

8/31/2007   Piersol Details

Jeff is now ensconced in his new private room, overlooking the beautiful University Museum, Franklin Field, and the skyline of Philadelphia.

Visiting hours are (technically) 11am - 8pm daily. The earlier hours of the day will be filled with therapy sessions, so it may be best to visit after 4pm. If he is working hard, he may be sleeping then, so visitors will have to take their chances.

When they moved him into the room, they weighed him. I said he was skinny? He weighs 155 lbs.! That means that he has 50 pounds to gain to reach his normal healthy weight. Let's see, if you had to gain 50 pounds, what would you eat???

xxoo M'ree
Organ Donors Save Lives

∞

9/15/2007   Rocket Launch

First, the summary: Jeff's long-ago PCP predicted it when they transferred Jeff to Piersol. He said that Jeff would "take off like a rocket". It happened. It really happened. Since he got there, his progress has been nothing short of mind-boggling to everyone.

Yesterday he weighed 160 pounds; he's gained five pounds already. He looks great, relatively. He feels good. Every day he's markedly better than the day before. On Friday, the Transplant Team had their regular meeting and decided that Jeff can most likely come home on Monday, September 24th. That's only 10 days away! Now the details...

Remaining health issues:

- His butt is still really sore. The one remaining pressure ulcer is healing, but very, very slowly. It's still about the size of a quarter. The rest of his bony bottom is very red and burns like fire most of the time. They are doing everything they can to relieve the irritation and heal the skin. It will resolve in time.

- His left shoulder is not working well. They've concluded that he probably pulled or tore his rotator cuff when he fell out of bed a while back. He was simply trying to stand up and rolled too far too fast. I didn't mention it at the time because it seemed inconsequential. It's now improving slowly, with therapy.

Nutrition:

- He had another barium swallow test on Thursday morning and finally passed it. Liquids could still present a problem, so they are taboo for now. Jeff made a deal with the Speech/Swallow Therapist: no pureed foods, provided that he feeds himself and eats as much as possible at each meal. He gets finely chopped food (like the texture of taco meat). His first meal was Thursday dinner. I wasn't there when he ate, but he pronounced it "excellent". He said that it tasted good and he ate it all. No vomiting afterwards. He had a cheese omelet for breakfast on Friday. I saw his lunch tray and it really looked good. Honestly. It was beautiful red tomato sauce with chopped meatballs on top of chopped noodles, and a mound of green chopped broccoli. Dessert was a cup of apple crisp with a fat, red strawberry on the top. Not like hospital food, at all. And away we go.

- Until he is getting total nutrition by mouth, they will continue his tube feeds. They are timing them so that he is hungry at mealtime. He eats, and then gets his tube feed. As his eating increases, the tube feeds will decrease. Finally, when they can discontinue the tube feeds, they will leave the tube in place for "a while" just in case. It's a surgical procedure to insert it, so they don't want to be doing it again.

- We can do tube feeding at home, if he still needs it by then.

- Yesterday he took all his meds by mouth, with applesauce.

Physical Abilities:

- He can just stand right up from a seated position. No more rocking and counting first.

- He can walk pretty far (with a walker) without assistance. He knows how to pace himself and stops to rest when he needs it.

- He can walk up and down five 6" high stairs.

- He can get into bed and lift his legs in. He can roll from side to side in the bed. He can get his legs off the bed in preparation for sitting up. The only thing he can't do yet is raise his body from there without some assistance.

- He can get into and out of a shower set up to be like the one we have home, with a step-over entrance.

- He can move himself with a manual wheelchair. We will likely rent one for the time being so we can go to places like the movies and the grocery store. It will have an air cushion seat.

- Next week we will practice getting into and out of the car. Getting out will be a big challenge, but I believe he's up to it.

- He can put on his socks and shoes with the combination of a sock-putter-onner, a grabber and a long-handled shoehorn. He can put on and take off his shirt. He's working on the pants.

- They will give him extra therapy every day until his discharge.

Today I'm going to HUP very early and we're going to practice the whole wake up, bathroom and dress routine. He won't need a hospital bed at home, so we can put the bedroom furniture back where it belongs. He will have home PT and OT, and maybe outpatient, too. He still has a long way to go to relatively normal functioning and endurance.

He is pretty anxious about coming home: wondering if he will remember it and if he will be able to do what he needs to do. Can you even try to imagine what it's been like for him to have been totally dependent for seven months? Everyone reassures him that they won't let him out until he's absolutely ready, and that he will have all the help he needs at home. I can hardly wait!

xxoo M'ree
Organ Donors Save Lives

9/20/2007　Rehearsing a Fall Dinner Date

Yesterday Jeff achieved a huge goal: he got into and out of the car without assistance. You should have seen the look of utter relief on his face as he said, "That wasn't so bad." He was very anxious about doing this because the last attempt, while still at BMR, was a big struggle and resulted in him being unable to get out without three people helping. I kept reminding him that his ascites belly was like a nine-month pregnancy then, plus he was ill and weak, but he was still worried. No more. This means that I will drive him home on Monday; no ambulance needed.

Another big item: the Physical Therapist said that he no longer clinically needs a wheelchair, so we decided that we will not order a rental. If it turns out that we really need it for whatever reason, we can get one. He can't walk long distances yet, so we will just plan accordingly. And I'm going to ask the Physical Therapist about getting a special seat cushion to use in the car and on chairs.

Then, after the car trial, Jeff was back in PT practicing his walking. I was with him, at his left (weaker) side. He was starting to turn right when he turned his body before turning the walker and he lost his balance. You know how those things happen in slow motion. I saw him starting to spin and was able to break his fall, but not stop it. Boom. Right on his sore butt. Therapists came running and they called the doctor to check Jeff out. He was fine, except for being embarrassed. We did an instant replay for Jeff, with me playing him and the Physical Therapist playing me. He learned to always stay within the boundaries of the walker. I learned how to grab him by the hip and pull him to me to help keep his balance without falling over myself. Good lessons to learn there vs on the outside. He had no bruises yesterday, but there was a little bleeding from his pressure ulcer. He will likely be sore today.

Next big item: his eating and drinking is now unrestricted. So we had a dinner date. They brought his tray and I went to the cafeteria to get soup for both of us. He sat on the edge of the bed and I was in a chair with the rolling bed tray as our table. It was actually fun. Our plan for the weekend is to take him to the cafeteria for lunch each day. His supplemental tube feeds happen overnight.

Talk about approach-avoidance. Jeff is so ready and longing to come home, but he is still so afraid. I hope that as he gets stronger each day his fear will lessen.

That Team of Angels has sure done one heavenly job.

xxoo M'ree
Organ Donors Save Lives

∞

9/25/2007   Two Hundred Twenty-One and Done

Time to celebrate: he's home at last, for the first time since February 16th.   And, oh, how I wish it were as simple as you might think. The process of restarting his life at home is not easy and it won't be over for a long time, either.

I arrived at HUP before 8am, anticipating a discharge by 11am as they told us to expect (Didn't I know better than that?). The Attending Physician had rounded before my arrival. Jeff was already awake and dressed and impatient to get going. We had visits from the Piersol MD and the Nutritionist. Jeff's Nurse gave me training on wound care and tube feeding. A representative from Therapy arrived with a laminated "Certificate of Completion" for Jeff, which touched him. I packed up his remaining stuff. Then we waited. And waited. Then we had a lunch date. Then we waited some more. Finally, at 2:30pm, Jeff's Nurse arrived with all the discharge papers; there was so much it was in a bulging pocket folder. She reviewed it all with me and then gave us the ok to go. There were a lot of happy tears all around. The transport person pushed the wheelchair across the bridge to the parking lot and Jeff got into the car just so smoothly. We both enjoyed the ride home, except that Jeff's butt was uncomfortable even with the pillow I brought. That will take a while to get back to normal. We got home at 4pm. Then the rushing about began in earnest.

I parked up on the level of the back door and ran inside for the walker. With that, Jeff was able to get out of the car and into the house like a pro with only a couple of short stops to catch his breath. He wanted to lie down, so we went into the bedroom to get him into the brand new clean sheets I had installed before I left for HUP. Of course, for the first time ever, one of the cats had thrown up in the middle of the bed, so I got to strip and remake the whole thing. They must have believed he had run away from home, never to return. Maybe they wanted to give him a welcome home gift.

Then the phone started. The delivery person was coming with the feeding pump and the food, and the rest of the feeding supplies. The Nutrition Nurse was coming after that to set us up and do more training. A second nurse, who will be our regular Visiting Nurse, had intended to come, too, but it was too late in the day. She's coming tomorrow morning.

Next I had to get to the pharmacy to fill the dozen-odd prescriptions we needed to start right away. First I had to get out all of the drugs that we had from pre-transplant and also the ones we were given when Jeff first left HUP (and which he had never used). I compared them to what he now needs and purged those that were no longer needed. Meanwhile, I installed Jeff lying down on the living room sofa.

The pharmacy trip took a good while, and it wasn't simple, either. They were lacking two of the meds. One will be ready later today. The other was unavailable in a few pharmacies, but the pharmacist finally found some at a store a few miles down the road. Luckily, they were open until 10pm, which was a good thing because I had to get home to meet the Nutrition Nurse. The bad news is that I wasn't familiar with the generic name of one of the drugs. Turns out I discarded a bunch of that one and it was one we still needed. Whatever.

When I got back home, the delivery person was waiting outside. His dispatcher neglected to tell him I was leaving the door open since I would be out and Jeff would be on the sofa, still unable to get himself up or respond in any way. Now we have a stack of large cartons in the dining room and bags of associated stuff piled around that. Before he left, the Nutrition Nurse arrived. She had started her career as an ICU nurse and was just terrific. She trained both of us, and then started the pump, then got Jeff ensconced in the bed, propped up to 30 degrees with lots of pillows. She stayed with him while I went to the other pharmacy to get the missing drug. When I got back, Jeff was not comfortable at all, so we decided to move back to the living room. The Nutrition Nurse stayed a while longer, then she left and we ate dinner. That was enough to calm the both of us since we were both exhausted physically, mentally and emotionally. I put Jeff to bed and went to sleep on the sofa.

I woke to the beeping of the pump, which somehow had malfunctioned. Jeff was sleeping through the beeping. I got it working and went back to the sofa. More beeping. This time Jeff woke up, so we ended up on the phone with the support person, who concluded the pump is probably bad and is sending another one later today. If he were not eating anything orally, they would have sent someone immediately.

Tube feeds will continue probably for a couple of weeks, until it's certain Jeff has made really good progress in the nutrition department. He weighs 164.5 as of yesterday morning; he's gained about 10 pounds since August 31st. About 40 to go.

We have not yet heard from the Physical and Occupational Therapists who will be making regular visits. I guess they will call today and set up their schedules.

The living room and bedroom look like a cyclone hit them, which is not our favorite state. I'll tackle that today. The cats are sleeping around. Lover Boy slept with Jeff; Shadow slept with me. Things will return to normal step by step. We are both looking forward to seeing our friends again. We are so grateful for the prayers, messages, calls and visits from our friends and family. The journey continues.

xxoo M'ree
Organ Donors Save Lives

∞

10/6/2007   The New "Normal"

Allrighty then. He's been home for almost two weeks now and we are both settling into a sort-of routine. I'll tell you about the routine first, and then give the news.

The Drill: Jeff gets meds at 6am, 9am, 9pm and 10pm. There are about a dozen of them, but only a handful will continue long term. He gets a protein supplement (powder mixed into water and given through the G-tube) sometime during the day. Tube feeds will continue (via a pump we can wheel around the house with him), probably for "a couple of weeks", for 12 hours daily, starting at 6pm. In between, we get up, eat three meals (high protein, low sodium), get cleaned up and showered (showers not every day for Jeff), have visits from the Visiting Nurse (Mon, Wed and Fri), the Wound Care Nurse (once every two weeks), PT (Mon, Wed and Fri), and OT (Tues and Thurs).

Bathroom visits continue 24/7. We got a monitor, so while I'm upstairs working, I can be sure to hear him when he needs me.

We are scheduled for home care visits three times a week for an hour, but they haven't started yet. Our intention is to use that person for assistance with Jeff's showering. Jeff is ok with that and it will save me time. Then, of course, there is laundry (lots of that), trash (tons of that), errands, etc. Never having had a baby, I can only imagine that this is something like coming home with your first child. Now I really understand why, long ago, a nurse told me to get my rest while he was in HUP because I would not get it later. The worst trial is the many sleep interruptions overnight. We are both chronically over-tired and I am seriously sleep-deprived.

News: Jeff looks absolutely great overall. His skin is much less dry and the many bruises are starting to disappear. The skin tears are almost healed, and it's rare that he gets another. He is gaining weight like a tournament eater: he's up to over 170 pounds, with about 30 more to go.

He is also starting to get edema in his feet and ankles for whatever reason. We're working on remedies and the Transplant Team wants to avoid diuretics for the moment. Unfortunately, he pulled a muscle on his middle right side, so he is taking pain meds as needed and his mobility is restricted. This will slow him down, but he's doing many exercises for his muscles. He is walking very smoothly with the walker, but isn't ready to go without it. He still cannot sit from a horizontal position. He stands with only a little help from a seated position. The OT person suggested "bed lifts" for the sofa and two large living room chairs. They are sturdy blocks that fit under each leg of the bed (or chair) and elevate it five inches. They are sold at major linen stores, and are intended to add storage space in college dorm rooms. We got them and they make it much easier for Jeff to sit down because of the added height.

His first outpatient HUP Liver Transplant checkup was on Tuesday. We got him into the car, to HUP, into a wheelchair, to the clinic, onto the exam table, back into the wheelchair, back into the car, home and back to bed. It was tiring for him, but he managed really well. The Transplant Team just oohed and aahed over how well he is doing. The next appointment will be on the 16th, then going forward they will reduce in frequency. In between, the Visiting Nurse will draw blood for labs every week. Anyway, he really enjoyed the car ride down and back; it made him feel part of the world again. We took the long, scenic, way home to give him a treat. The OT person told us that insurance considers Jeff to be "home bound", which means that he should only be going out for doctor's appointments. We should minimize anything else for the time being, at least while home nurse and therapy visits continue. That's fine, because he still has essentially no stamina.

The annoying highlight of the week was after I had to go to my local office for a few hours on Wednesday. I arranged for a Home Care Nurse while I was gone. Without knowing any better, she double locked our dining room door, which we never lock. The next day when I innocently closed the door to take out the trash, you know what happened. Jeff was totally unable to help, so I had to break a pane of glass in the greenhouse to get back in. At least I thought strategically enough to break one that was already cracked from a branch or whatever hitting it. Then I had to go to Lowe's for a piece of Plexiglas to temporarily replace it. It's like a Neil Simon movie.

And so the recovery is well under way. Jeff loves hearing from everyone. Life is good, well, better.

xxoo M'ree
Organ Donors Save Lives

∞

10/16/2007 Update After Doctor's Appointments

Lots of news, almost all excellent; nothing is bad. This is stream of consciousness.

His liver is still working perfectly. He weighed 178 pounds at HUP.

Tube feeds can be stopped any time. We have eight days' worth of supplies remaining. We're not doing one tonight, as John and Penny are coming. We're not doing them Friday, Saturday and Sunday, because Christy and her husband, Robin, will be here. Otherwise, we will just use it up. Then we watch to see that he keeps up his oral nutrition and a slow, steady weight gain. Assuming he does, the tube will be removed in a number of weeks. I have to be the sodium police, which won't be fun since Jeff so loves salty foods.

We are discontinuing all non-transplant meds, with the exclusion of the anti-depressant, since there is no way to tell whether he's actually not depressed anymore, or whether he is but the drug is working. We will revisit that one in a couple of months, since it does no harm to take it. The PCP added a mild diuretic, to resolve the slight foot/ankle edema. He should start taking a multi-vitamin daily.

He can continue to take the pain med as needed for the pulled muscle (which is slowly improving). He's technically on 5mgs every 4-6 hours. Sometimes he doesn't ask for it that often. The PCP said that he can take more if he needs it, but not more than 30mgs at a time. He said not to worry; he won't let Jeff become addicted.

He will have a DexaScan on October 24th. This is a bone density test, which is standard for anyone who is on immuno-suppressants (or menopausal women, to check for osteoporosis).

His next appointment with his PCP is on November 19th. His next liver transplant appointment is on December 11th. He needs to have blood drawn monthly for standard liver function tests.

He should continue his periodic colonoscopies as usual, as well as his annual dermatologist appointments.

I don't know how long the Visiting Nurse, Wound Care Nurse, PT and OT visits will continue. Time will tell. As soon as his pulled back muscle permits, he must resume his strength and endurance work.

That's the whole scoop.

No it isn't. Two things I forgot:

First, he is slightly anemic. This is a common side effect of the other drugs he is on. It's not concerning at this slight level and they will not treat it. It is not an iron deficiency anemia, and iron supplements would not affect it. They will continue to watch it.

Second, when we arrived at the Transplant Center yesterday, we were very warmly greeted by one of Jeff's best Nurse Assistants during the long time in the SICU. About a week before Jeff was released from the SICU, she wasn't there. I asked where she was, and they told me that she had hurt her back pretty badly helping an uncooperative patient. We never saw her again. Well, she's back on "light duty" escorting patients around in the Transplant Center. She gushed on and on about how great Jeff looks and was amazed to see him stand up and walk a little. It made her feel so good to see one of her patients who were recovering; I guess that doesn't happen often. Of course, Jeff didn't remember her, but he was touched when we explained it. He's starting to get some little insights into what he went through.

xxoo M'ree
Organ Donors Save Lives

∞

10/27/2007 One Month Out

After one full month at home, Jeff is continuing his recovery at a steady pace. Our daily routine has simplified and he needs less assistance from me. Life is seeming much more like the old days.

His general condition: Jeff's pulled back muscle seems to be almost totally resolved. He still has general muscle soreness, but needs few pain meds. He is getting markedly stronger every day in terms of both muscle strength and stamina. The one remaining deficit is that he still can't sit up from a prone position, but even that is getting close. He can both sit and stand without help. He can walk extremely well with the walker, and even a little without it. His balance is not good enough, nor reliable enough, to eliminate the walker yet. He gets into and out of the car unaided. We still need the "bed lifters" on the sofa and wing-back chair, as well as the toilet seat booster, because he has trouble sitting on and getting up from a low seat. He still has the shower chair, but will not need that for much longer. He is still not comfortable sitting for any length of time, because his butt is so skinny. He is not depressed. We don't know whether he's really not depressed, or whether he is still depressed but the anti-depressant is working. He still sleeps a lot of the time. We are still getting up multiple times during the night, but the bathroom trips are easier and shorter. He is not bored yet.

Meds and Nutrition: The number of meds has decreased so that he only takes them in the morning and at night. He's now on a diuretic, because he has developed some ankle and foot edema. He still gets the daily protein supplement via the PEG tube. We will stop that when it runs out, which should be another two weeks or so. The last tube feed ended this morning; they will pick up the pump on

Monday. It was never a problem, but it was a big production, so we are very glad to see it go. Now we have to watch his weight to be sure he is slowly and steadily gaining. Jeff's PCP told us to expect that he will initially lose some weight due to the combination of the diuretic, eliminating the tube feeds, and increased activity. He has, in fact, already lost a few pounds. It will be some weeks until they remove the PEG tube; they want to be sure they don't have to reinsert it. His appetite is very good and he's getting lots of protein at every meal. Unfortunately, he still craves salt. I was hopeful that since he had zero for such a long time, he would have lost his taste for it. Anyway, his sodium should be under 2000 mgs/day, so I have to remind him sometimes. I hate telling him he can't have something he wants, but, guess what? The b---h is back.

Health Care Visits: The Visiting Nurse will now come only twice a week. PT will likely continue at three times weekly, and OT at twice. The Wound Care Nurse came today and pronounced his pressure ulcer so healed from the Promogran (high-tech wound bandage thingy) that we don't need that any more. From here on we will just use the Allevin: it looks exactly like a square Band-Aid with adhesive all around, but the dressing part is really a foam substance that allows air to circulate while keeping the wound moist. She's coming back in one week.

Health Appointments: This week he had a DexaScan. We won't have the results for a couple of weeks. We both got flu shots, because getting the flu at this point would be disaster. He had a long-overdue tooth cleaning and one cavity was filled. Two more fillings are coming up. We have also scheduled his three-year colonoscopy, as well as his annual dermatology checkup. We intend, at some point, to have his eyes examined. We have appointments to take him back to the PCP in November and the Transplant Team in December.

TJ, Christy and Robin came for a few days. It was so great to have them here with Jeff so improved. They will be back, with TJ's wife, Ziva, and their boys, Zach and Noah, for Thanksgiving. We have a miracle to be thankful for this year.

xxoo M'ree
Organ Donors Save Lives

∞

11/20/2007 Almost Two Months Out

It's time for another update, as there is some very big news to report.

The biggest: the PEG tube, which was inserted on May 14th, will be removed on November 29th. Jeff had his last tube feed about three weeks ago and has been doing very well, thank you, without them. He now weighs 184.6 by our scale: up 29.6 pounds from his lowest. That puts him about 20 pounds below his healthy pre-transplant weight, but that will creep back in time. The tube has been causing him lots of general discomfort and he will be so glad when it's gone. Me, too: it still makes me cringe to see that tube dangling out of his belly. Just think: we will finally be able to give him regular hugs for the first time since way, way before the transplant.

Next, as of today he has been discharged from all home nursing and therapy. The pressure ulcer is totally healed, so the Wound Care Nurse stopped coming. His general health is so good that the Visiting Nurse stopped visiting. The Occupational Therapist had nothing more to teach him given his current state of physical ability. The Physical Therapist has gone as far as she could at the house. We have a prescription for outpatient PT, which we will do at a NovaCare rehab center very close to home. The evaluation appointment is set for Monday, December 3rd. PT will work on general strength and endurance, plus help with the left shoulder weakness from the old rotator cuff injury.

He can now sit up from a horizontal position almost every time. He still has the walker, but gets by with a cane in the house. Over the weekend, he took a whole shower without sitting on the shower chair. He didn't wash his legs or feet; did I care? He has started to do things in the kitchen, including get his own breakfast and help with cooking. He can't bend much at the waist, so there are the limitations you would expect in that department. He has not yet been up or down our 200+ year-old corkscrew stairs. That will have to wait until he is stronger and more stable on his feet.

Jeff saw his PCP on Monday. The PCP wants him back in a month, and said that before too long we will "stop the foolishness" of such frequent visits. His way of practicing medicine is nothing short of extraordinary. No wonder another doctor said Jeff won the lottery in getting this PCP.

Jeff complains of being cold all the time, which the PCP says is because he is missing his fat insulation layer. Also, he still has some edema in his feet, ankles and lower legs, which the PCP says will slowly go away as his general nutritional situation normalizes. He did have a short bout with c-diff again about a week ago, so he is on antibiotics for the time being. This is the first time since coming home that he's been "sick", if you can call that sick. The PCP says this is not uncommon.

The Social Worker called last evening for an ordinary social chat. She said that the staff from the SICU and the Transplant Floor and the Therapists always asks her how Jeff is doing. She said they are frustrated because they don't see their patients after they recover. She made us promise to visit all of them the next time we go to HUP so everyone can see for themselves what a terrific recovery Jeff has made. That date would be December 11th, his next Transplant checkup. It also happens to be the date of the annual Transplant Holiday Party, a bring-food-pot-luck event, full of tears and hugs and big smiles. We went last year and met a number of recipients and heard their stories. This year it will be a very different experience.

Jeff looks like his old self again, except that his pants are baggy. He sounds like his old self, too and his voice is strong. We look back to last year at this time when we didn't know how much sicker he would or could get, or how we would be able to hang on until he would eligible for transplant, or whether he would ever get a transplant. We both wonder how we got through it. Jeff is learning about things that happened while he was too sick to remember them. Even though we are both generally very tired, we are teeny step by teeny step getting back to what you could call normal. We are just thankful for where we are today and looking forward to tomorrow.

Savor Thanksgiving with those you love. This is the best holiday of all.

xxoo M'ree
Organ Donors Save Lives

∞

12/22/2007 Ex-Peg Tube

News develops all the time. Since the last update, just a short month ago, here it is.

The PEG tube is history. Note this, everyone: If you ever have a PEG tube and anyone wants to remove it without numbing you, tell them "NO" loud and clear. A resident just grabbed the tube close to Jeff's chest and quickly yanked it out with one strong tug. We had been told that this is what they do, but I assumed they were kidding, because you would need stitches to close the hole in your stomach and also in your skin, right? Wrong. The stomach heals the hole instantly and at the same time, forms a permanent bond with the skin. Nobody tells you that it hurts. A lot. Jeff has a very high pain tolerance, but his face immediately turned first absolutely white, and then scarlet, and he yelled something I can't include here. After a few minutes, the pain subsided and being the gentleman he is, he apologized for the epithet. But, you know, they deserved it. At any rate, it's over.

The biggest new news is that two weeks ago tomorrow, Jeff was kneeling (I don't know how he got into that position) in front of the fireplace, adding a small log, when he yelled and rolled over onto his back. He said he heard a loud crack, like popping a knuckle but louder. The fire was crackling, so I couldn't differentiate the sound. He said he saw stars and thought he broke his back. I knew better than to try to move him, so I let him decide what to do when. He moved his head, then his arms and legs. Everything worked, but his back really hurt. We got him up, slowly and carefully. Since then, he's been in a lot of pain and taking lots of pain meds, but it's gradually lessened. Heat helps. It's painful to sit, so mostly he lies down or walks gingerly. When he goes to PT, which he does twice a week, they work around it and give him helpful suggestions.

Yesterday we went to see Jeff's PCP. He examined Jeff thoroughly and pronounced that he has a compression fracture of the spine. And no wonder, either, because the recent DexaScan (bone scan of the spine and hip) results just came back, and Jeff has osteoporosis. So now Jeff will be taking a drug (endorsed on TV by Sally Field) for that. That should stop and even reverse his bone loss in time. Meanwhile, there is nothing to do about the fracture except wait for it to heal, apply heat and take pain meds. The PCP says it usually takes about six weeks.

Jeff is very slowly gaining weight, which is fine and good. He now weighs about 187 pounds more or less: a questionable number because of the edema in his lower legs, ankles and feet. The edema has been lessening, in part because his immune-suppressant dose was cut in half by the Transplant Team. This will be an ongoing balancing act. He is still supposed to severely restrict his sodium intake, of course.

From a physical perspective, he's very slowly making progress, even considering his back. He doesn't use the walker any more, but he does use his cane, which he calls his "stick". We aren't ready to give the walker away, though, in case we go somewhere it would make sense to have it. We did put away the shower chair. He hasn't been upstairs yet. That should be next.

We did have a big, big day during our last visit to HUP on December 11th. We got a wheelchair for the duration because we were going to cover more ground than Jeff would be able to manage. First was the regular transplant visit. Nothing remarkable there, except that everyone is impressed with how good he looks and how well he is coming along. We had lunch with the Social Worker. It was her first chance to "meet" Jeff as a walking and talking person. Then we went through HUP, from unit to unit, to each of the places where Jeff stayed. Everywhere we went, we got a huge welcome from the staff. Everyone was so clearly moved by seeing Jeff in a relatively healthy state, and was so grateful that we gave them that chance. The SICU was the highlight. Each one of the staff who knew us came rushing to greet us as soon as they could. Sarah, who had been his Primary Nurse, was crying, and we were, too. They whipped out a camera and took a group photo of us with them. They kept thanking us for visiting. They rarely get to see their patients after they leave. This must be so hard for them, given how much they invest in each one. After all that, we had intended to stay for the liver transplant holiday buffet party, but Jeff was totally spent so we made our apologies and left for home. Next year.

Speaking of next year, this one is almost at a close. We will be thrilled to kiss this one goodbye. Happy New Year everyone!

xxoo M'ree
Organ Donors Save Lives

∞

1/21/2008   Zig-Zag

We usually take "zig-zag" to mean sideways. In Nepal, it means "up and down", as in mountains. Jeff is in zig-zag mode now.

He was doing so well and making steady progress until he broke his back on December 9th. That put his recovery on hold because the pain is way too intense for him to do virtually anything. Even with his drugs, he pretty much has to be horizontal to keep the pain manageable. Also, he has lost his appetite; maybe that's from the drugs, too. The PCP says most compression fractures take 6-8 weeks to heal to the point that pain subsides. There is nothing else to do but wait. Jeff did get a home TENS machine from PT. If you haven't heard of them, a TENS is a Transcutaneous Electrical Nerve Stimulator: a battery-powered gizmo about the size of a pack of cigarettes that connects to electrodes you place around the pain site. It sends electrical pulses into your body that cause the nerves to relax. Jeff says the TENS doesn't actually relieve the pain, but it does distract his attention from it. Better than nothing, for sure. As time passes, he's getting more deconditioned. As of yesterday, he has lost 10 pounds. I try my best to tempt him with food he loves, but it's not working yet. We are both convinced that he will bounce back when the pain goes.

Then last Friday evening (a week ago) the phone rang. It was the HUP Transplant Coordinator. Jeff's most recent bloodwork showed that three of his liver enzymes have elevated quickly and enough to sound the alarm for possible liver rejection. That was a real shock and just the thought of it hit Jeff very hard. My auto-pilot immediately turned on. We had to change his immuno-suppressant meds immediately and go back to HUP on Monday for a liver biopsy. The biopsy isn't too bad in itself, but since the liver is a bloody organ and they need to prevent internal bleeding, you have to lie absolutely still on your side for three hours afterwards and then lie still on your back for another hour. Oh, no. Not a good thing for his back. His back pain was so bad in the recovery room that they shot him with something and it took a doctor and a nurse and me to get him up off the gurney. At home, his pain just got worse and worse as the hours passed. We called HUP in the middle of the night. They said to get him to the ER for IV pain control. He said NO. Finally, at 4am, he gave in and we went.

We were in the ER for 11 hours and they kept him gorked on pain meds. While we were there, they did a CAT scan which showed that the biopsy site itself was just fine and there was no excess internal bleeding. Also, we learned that the biopsy showed *no organ rejection*. Hooray! It did show, though, that there is something going on. It may be a virus, or maybe a reoccurrence of the original auto-immune disorder that caused his liver to fail after so many years. We were all sort of expecting that, because since they never diagnosed it, they surely hadn't eliminated it. Since it took so long for his first liver to fail, the expectation is that the new one will most likely last for the rest of his natural life. So we are back to chemistry. They adjusted his meds again and took lots of blood to diagnose the situation further. We are awaiting results.

Just to be clear, if there were any rejection, it can be slight or severe and it does not have to lead to complete organ failure. If it's slight, they just adjust or change meds. If severe, they would admit him to HUP for a few days of IV steroids. Rejection can happen at any time, which is why they do periodic blood tests and why he will take some amount of anti-rejection drugs forever. Welcome to post-transplant life.

xxoo M'ree
Organ Donors Save Lives

∞

2/14/2008   One Year Out

It's both dragged and flown. February 16th will be one whole year since Jeff's admission to HUP. It's a serious blessing that we had no way to know at the time what was to come. Now both of us find ourselves slowly recovering from the mind-boggling physical and emotional experience of his transplant and the aftermath. So many people have said to me that they don't know how I did it. My response always was and still is that anyone can do it; you just don't realize it until it's your turn. Now, though, looking back, I absolutely do not know how either of us did it. The whole thing seems impossible to fathom, so I don't go there.

Anyway, here we are. Jeff's rate of recovery was picking up again until last weekend, when he fell in the kitchen. I left him having breakfast to restack some firewood in the yard. When I came inside, his cane was on the floor, he clearly hadn't eaten, and there was a huge swollen piece of toast floating in the cats' water bowl. When I got to the bedroom, there he was in bed, clearly in a lot of pain. He says he tried to pick up the toast, lost his balance and went down somehow; he can't recall the details. He crawled to a dining room chair, got himself standing, and went to bed. Nothing broken, just very sore. Since then, he had a few days unable to get to a seated position without my help - remember that phase? Now he's regained that facility, but he's still taking plenty of pain meds. His twice weekly PT didn't miss a beat. They just reset the program to the days after he broke his back. Can you believe this?

Anyway, an anniversary is time for celebration, so I've planned a fantasy hospital-style dinner party for Saturday night. Here's the menu:

Hors D'Oeuvres

Pureed Chicken Livers on low-sodium saltines

Soup

Low-sodium Chicken Broth

Entrée

Pureed Calves Liver and Onions

Mashed Powdered Potatoes with butter substitute

Pureed Carrots

Desert

Sugar-free Lime Jell-O blocks

Unsweetened Applesauce

Beverages

Cranberry Juice

Non-fat Milk

Sugar-free Ginger Ale

Decaf Coffee and Tea

Sound just yummy to you?

xxoo M'ree
Organ Donors Save Lives

∞

6/18/2008   Wednesday Drive

It's official. Jeff is permitted to drive a car after the almost 1 1/2-year break. On Monday, armed with a prescription written by Jeff's PCP, we went to Moss Rehab Hospital's Driving School. We never knew that there is a program designed to assess the ability to drive a car. It's for all sorts of people, but, in Jeff's case, for those who have had a prolonged illness. The "instructor" made me sit in the waiting room while he took Jeff into the back for tests of his comprehension and vision, as well as reflexes, which they test with a dummy "car" gizmo.

Then he took Jeff out for a spin in a real dual-control car. It took about 1 1/2 hours. When they returned, he included me in the assessment. He said that he's sending a report to the PCP stating that Jeff is now permitted to drive. He did say that there were a couple of times when Jeff goofed with directions, but he thinks that was just because a lot was going on, and he's not telling the PCP. (Jeff did say later that he kept up a steady stream of conversation; I think that was part of the test.) He said that I should be in the car with Jeff for a while, and that there should be no long trips at first. That's fine with us. Today, Jeff drove me to the post office. I felt like a queen!

Also, we got good news a week ago when we went for Jeff's

quarterly HUP Transplant Team appointment. From now on, we only have to visit them every six months. And, in between, instead of monthly, he only needs to have his blood drawn every other month. And, as if that's not enough, today they called with lab results from last week, and they are cutting his oral steroid dose in half. That's super, because the steroid (which he takes for the auto-immune disorder that caused the liver failure in the first place and has now returned) is what is making his skin so thin and sensitive. Maybe he will be more comfortable overall.

We are still waiting for the insurance company's ok to continue the PT that the Therapists recommend for another three months. They said his trunk muscles need strengthening, as do his legs. His back still hurts when he makes certain movements. His energy level is still very, very low and he sleeps a lot. He still walks slowly and wobbles. But he's coming back. At long last.

Phone calls are a joy for him. He loves to talk.

xxoo M'ree
Organ Donors Save Lives

7 EPILOGUE

Jeff's recovery continued for four more years. It was slow but sure, with setbacks along the way, some minor, some definitely major.

There was the systemic fungal infection that originated with his feeding tube. That required a short hospitalization, with months of subsequent drug therapy and visits to the Ophthalmologist since it had gotten into his eyes. Fortunately, it never reached his heart, which would have been catastrophic.

There was the large abdominal hernia that appeared, to our dismay. They weren't about to open his belly again, so he just lived with it.

There were a few scary rejection false alarms, requiring liver biopsies. We lived under the shadow of his original autoimmune disorder, which was never identified or cured. We knew it would inevitably return but avoided thinking about it because what would be, would be. What to do? Nothing. We just hoped that if it was the original disease, it would come back very slowly, as it had in the first place, so he would live a long life with his donated liver.

Then there was the PTLD, Post-Transplant Lymphoproliferative Disorder (a form of Lymphoma). It happens with some transplant recipients because of being immunosuppressed. It came on fast. He had many outpatient chemo sessions. He was lucky that the drugs didn't cause the dreaded nausea, but he did lose what was left of his hair. Then, two months after the PTLD was gone, it returned with a vengeance. They could offer only one option: "salvage chemo". This is a drastic process, with chemo so strong that it could possibly kill him. To avoid death, the first step is harvesting white blood cells from the patient so they can infuse them back after the chemo to encourage recovery. Usually this is done via a series of outpatient procedures, but, Jeff's system being Jeff's system, his white cells were "hiding" and they couldn't get nearly enough. So they had to do it surgically. He was hospitalized for three weeks. First the white cell harvesting. Then the chemo. Then the white cell infusions. Then the slow recovery. It worked, which was a good thing, because that was THE last resort.

Then, given the PTLD episodes, the decision was made to cease Jeff's autoimmune suppressant and anti-rejection drug therapies. Everyone involved held their collective breath while I staved off a panic attack, waiting to see whether his new liver would now fail. But by now you know that whatever is expected won't happen with Jeff. And, true to that tradition, his new liver just kept on functioning just fine. It seems there are some transplant recipients who live without those drugs, for whatever reasons.

Then Jeff's blood test results showed that his original autoimmune disorder was slowly but surely returning. It could just stop in its tracks, it could take 20 years or more for his liver to fail, or it could move fast. There would not be another transplant. We didn't talk about how bad it would surely get before the end.

Such very special things happened in Jeff's last four years. He spent time with his kids, grandsons, and his friends. He did have that toot of single malt with his friend, John. He worked with the horses again and even helped on a carriage drive. He sailed again. He actually went to work for a few months. We visited his alma mater in Conway, Arkansas, and then drove through the beautiful southern countryside to New Orleans for a tour of the Tabasco factory at Avery Island and way too much outstanding food. We returned to Monhegan Island (where we were married after seven years of living together) for our 10th wedding anniversary. We stayed in the same cabin and feasted on lobster and mussels, plus champagne, of course. Those days were so sweet. And the view of Monhegan from the top of Manana was- well, maybe you can see it for yourself someday.

Then came the Christmas season of 2012. Jeff and I always wanted to hang a four-foot wreath on the outside of the house, so we finally got around to it. While he was coming down on the ladder I was bracing, he just let go on the next to the last rung, slowly fell backwards, and hit his head on the stone wall. The helicopter flew him to HUP. The many teams of doctors concluded he had "an event" on the ladder. They tried their absolute best, but it was simply Jeff's time to go. At his memorial service, one of his friends blew "Amazing Grace" on the coach horn. His ashes are buried on a hill at the farm, near the horses he loved. The void in my life is immense, but I am still standing.

Words could never be adequate to thank the donor's family for the ultimate gift of life for five years, nine months and two gloriously full days, when Jeff got to do again so many things he never thought he would.

And, oh, the brilliant, caring and selfless people of The Hospital of the University of Pennsylvania. The surgeons and doctors of all kinds. The nurses. The social workers. The therapists. The pharmacists and lab technicians. The nutritionists and dieticians. Those who clean the rooms, cook and deliver the meals, shuttle the patients from place to place, run the cafeteria, do the laundry, maintain the buildings, and provide security. The many I have neglected to mention. And the numerous home health professionals. You are all heroes to me.

Finally, let me not forget the merciful Team of Angels, who spared Jeff, me, Christy, and TJ from what was lurking around the corner.

ABOUT THE AUTHOR

Marie spent her 50-year professional career in facets of Information Technology, beginning with software development, then consulting, training, marketing, and finally in corporate recruiting. She is now volunteering for very worthy causes. This is her first book. Who knows whether it will be her last?

Her avocations include walking, fine films, knitting, cooking, photography, and travel to out-of-the-way places. She and her cat, Lover Boy, are now putting one foot / paw in front of the other on California's Monterey Peninsula, ready for whatever life has in store.

Made in the USA
Coppell, TX
03 November 2021